Evolutionary Games and Poverty Traps

Evolutionary Games and Poverty Traps

By

Edgar J. Sánchez Carrera

Evolutionary Games and Poverty Traps

By Edgar J. Sánchez Carrera

This book first published 2016

Cambridge Scholars Publishing

Lady Stephenson Library, Newcastle upon Tyne, NE6 2PA, UK

British Library Cataloguing in Publication Data
A catalogue record for this book is available from the British Library

ISBN (10): 1-4438-8516-9
ISBN (13): 978-1-4438-8516-4

DEDICATION

This book is dedicated to my wife Laura, my children Matteo and Pietro, and my mother Yolanda Carrera.

To my father Miguel Angel, and my brothers Mayo and Luis.

Because they are all the love in my life!

CONTENTS

List of Figures ix

Preface xi

Chapter One 1
Introduction: Evolutionary Poverty Traps
1.1. Learning by Imitation
1.2. High Profile Economic Agents
1.3. Strategic Behavior of Economic Agents
1.4. Outline

Chapter Two 17
Evolutionary Games
2.1. Strategic Game
2.2. Population Game
2.3 On the Notion of ESS in Asymmetric Games
2.4. The Replicator Dynamics

Chapter Three 39
Imitation in Two Asymmetric Populations
3.1. The Model
3.2. Imitation by Dissatisfaction
3.3. Adopting the Most Successful Strategy
3.4. Evolutionarily Stable Strategies
3.5. The Specific Behavioral Rule
3.6. Concluding Remarks

Chapter Four 59
The Evolution of Poverty Traps
4.1. The Game
4.2. The Evolutionary Game
4.3. ESSs and Evolutionary Dynamics
4.4 To Overcome the Poverty Trap
4.5 Concluding Remarks

Chapter Five 77
Evolution and Complementarities of Firms and Workers
5.1. The Game
5.2. Dynamic Imitation of Workers
5.3. Initial Conditions Matter
5.4. Dynamic Equilibria and Nash Equilibria
5.5. Concluding Remarks

Chapter Six 99
The Replicator Dynamics for Firms and Workers
6.1. The Replicator by Imitation
6.1.1 The Specific Behavioral Rule
6.1.2 Stability and Equilibria Analysis
6.1.3 How to Overcome a Poverty Trap: Going for Education Costs
6.2 Replicator Dynamics with Fiscal Incentives
6.3 Concluding Remarks

Chapter Seven.. 113
Economic Agents and Development
7.2. On the Evolutionary Dynamics
7.3 Concluding Remarks

Bibliography 127

LIST OF FIGURES

Figure 3-1. Solution orbits from $\left(\dot{x}_c^R, \dot{x}_c^M\right)$.

Figure 4-1. Evolutionary dynamics driven by imitative behavior.

Figure 5-1. Convergence of high-skilled workers: above and below the threshold value.

Figure 5-2. Decreasing marginal costs for the innovative firms.

Figure 5-3. Dynamic evolution of firms from above and below the threshold level.

Figure 6-1. Vector field of the replicator system $\left(\dot{y}_I, \dot{x}_S\right)$.

Figure 6-2. Decreasing the G-value through education costs, skill premia and payoff taxation.

Figure 7-1. Nullclines intersect at $[0,1]\times[0,1]$.

Figure 7-2. Nullclines a-left and b-right do not intersect at $[0,1]\times[0,1]$.

PREFACE

Contemporaneous growth theory is especially interested in explaining why some countries grow and flourish while other countries appear to stagnate and not grow at all. Explaining growth as endogenous to agents' decisions and explaining very different growth paths across countries make it natural to consider the political economy of growth. Political Economy models attempt to explain economy growth outcome as reflecting endogenous political decisions. Accumulation of physical and human capital should be significantly affected by political decisions, so political economy of growth naturally fits in endogenous growth theory. In this work, we are particularly interested in explaining the influence of political decisions on the agents' decisions. We will analyze poverty traps as a state of stagnation in the growth of an economy, and the possibility of overcoming them through correct policy decisions that are reflected in correct and rational choices made by rational economic agents. However, in this work, we do not follow a standard approach. Our main tool is evolutionary game theory. The economic agents, attempting to maximize their own expectations, and looking at the behavior of institutions and that of other individuals, choose their own behavior. In this sense our analysis rises from the behavior of the economic agents.

Standard growth theory teaches us that poverty traps are stable-low level balanced growth paths to which economies gravitate due to adverse initial conditions or poor equilibrium selection. In other words, societies fail to take off into sustained growth because they started poor (e.g., low longevity or poor human capital as in Azariadis and Drazen, 1990), or because they cannot create institutions that coordinate their investments successfully. This thesis explains this pernicious form of coordination failure as a game between economic agents: leaders and followers investing to become high-profile. Rates of return of high-profile leaders depend on average high-profile followers (i.e. human capital), and rates of return on high-profile followers depend on aggregate high-profile leaders' investments (i.e. innovative firms or R&D). The outcome is a self-confirming equilibrium in evolutionarily stable strategies in which unsuccessful players imitate successful ones. This equilibrium has the following interesting property:

> *In poor economies with a large fraction of low-profile followers or low-profile leaders, imitative strategies do not support a take-off into sustained growth. To achieve that take-off, the society should subsidize the cost of education and/or skill premia through a tax system on income until the economy builds a critical mass of high-profile economic agents.*

Hence, we consider a baseline model in which we apply two different imitation rules. The baseline model studies an evolutionary game with two asymmetric populations where players from each population are paired with members of the other population. We consider imitation as the facilitator of evolutionary dynamics, resulting in evolutionarily stable strategies. We present two imitation models. In the first model, dissatisfaction drives imitation. In the second model, agents imitate the successful. In the first model, we use a simple reviewing rule, while in the second model, we use a proportional imitation rule where switching depends on agents comparing their payoffs to others' payoffs. We show that such imitation is approximated by a replicator dynamic system, following which we apply the well-known relationships between stability of stationary states, evolutionarily stable strategies (ESS), and Nash equilibria. We characterize the evolutionarily stable strategies of our two asymmetric populations and we show that a mixed strategy profile distribution of inhabitants can be an ESS if it is the strict Nash equilibrium. We offer one clear conclusion: whom an agent imitates is more important than how an agent imitates.

To reach our results, in this essay, we considered that the imitative behavior of the economic agents is the facilitator of the evolutionary dynamics of the economy, with this resulting in evolutionarily stable strategies.

So, this work applies evolutionary game theory to several models concerning the notions of economic agents and poverty traps. That is:

First, a coordination game interpreted as a game between economic agents; namely a leader and a follower. The leader must hire the follower and each player can be either a high or a low profile economic agent. The follower can decide to become the high profile type by incurring some training costs. Both players must also pay some income tax. A play that is stuck in the low-level or inefficient equilibrium is interpreted as being in a poverty trap. Self-confirming equilibria are analyzed before looking at the replicator dynamics driven by imitation. We show that the economy can be located in a low-level or high-level equilibrium, both of which are evolutionarily stable strategies against the field. Furthermore, we show that to overcome the poverty trap, there exists a threshold number of high-profile economic agents which depends mainly on training costs (or education costs), skill premia or bonuses for skillful agents, and income taxes.

Second, an economy with two types of firms (innovative and non-innovative) and two types of workers (high-skilled and low-skilled), where the workers' decisions are driven by imitative behavior, while firms' decisions depend on the number of high-skilled workers. We show that such an economy's evolution depends on the initial distribution of the firms. The multiple equilibria of this model can be characterized either by a continuum of high level steady states or only one low level steady state, for which there exists a threshold level to be overcome in order to attain the higher level equilibria. We show that in each high level equilibrium, a percentage of innovative firms coexist with a percentage of non-innovative firms, and a set of high-skilled workers coexist with a set of low-skilled workers. But if the initial percentage of innovative firms is lower than the threshold value, then the economy devolves to a low level equilibrium wholly composed of non-innovative firms and low-skilled workers.

Third, we consider that the decisions of both firms and workers are driven by imitating successful strategies. Firms and workers should decide whether to be high-profile or low-profile agents by following an imitative behavioral rule given the current state of the economy, characterized by the distribution of strategies. We apply evolutionary game theory to find the system of replicator dynamics, and characterize the low-level and high-level equilibria as evolutionarily stable strategies (ESSF) against the field. We introduce this concept to analyze the magnitude of change required in the initial conditions for this to be effective as an incentive for change in the attitude of the agents. In some ways, the measures are something very close to the inertia of a body in movement. We show that when the current state of the economy is in the basin of attraction of the poverty trap, players should play against the field "if they want to change the *status quo*". The threshold level to overcome the poverty trap can be lowered if there is an appropriate policy using income taxes, education costs and skill premia.

Moreover, as it is well known, individual income depends on both the education of the workers and the salary paid at each education level. The question about what happened in Mexico makes sense, where the export-manufacturing industries (maquiladoras), opened in the country after the implementation of the NAFTA, pay higher wages compared to domestic firms (see Harrison, and Lypsey (1996). The high salaries pulled workers out of school at younger ages, inhibiting their skill acquisition (for an interesting study analyzing this topic, see D. Atkin, 2010). So, nevertheless, the improvement in employment levels and the rising wages in the country that the establishment of these firms has implied are not the source of sustainable growth that the country requires, because they do not employ highly skilled workers. In many cases, it is domestic high-tech firms that play this role. Students may choose to stay in school for longer, but only if the firm will reward the additional skill acquisition. Therefore, we study the replicator dynamics with Pigovian subsidy and payoff taxation as a mechanism of equilibrium selection to overcome the poverty trap.

Fourth, this essay studies the dynamic complementarities of non-homogeneous firms and workers that face some costs and skill-biased technical change. We show that the profits of innovative firms increases as the supply of skilled workers increases by decreasing production costs and even lowering prices, all of this through time. There is a threshold of the share of skilled workers such that a firm prefers to be innovative than non-innovative. On the other hand, workers follow an imitative behavior to choose their skill profile. We show that, as the share of innovative firms is large enough, then the share of skilled workers in equilibrium depends to the reviewing rate of those unskilled workers. Moreover, the Mexican government intervention is justified only by the given incentives to the non-innovative firms to become innovative, with the objective of increasing the share of innovative firms, but once the economy is in the path of a high equilibrium, such an intervention should be canceled.

Finally, I really want to acknowledge to Elvio Accinelli and Lionello Punzo, since they gave me a taste for economic theory and the theory of games as a tool to understand the strategic foundations of economic growth and development. I am also indebted to Costas Azariadis, Samuel Bowles and Herbert Gintis for their helpful comments and frequent guidance to improve this research. To the faculty members of the Department of Economics at the University of Siena. To Facultad de Economia UASLP and FAI 2015 at UASLP Mexico for their financial support.

CHAPTER ONE

INTRODUCTION: EVOLUTIONARY POVERTY TRAPS

Economists have used the idea of economic agents to conceive of agents as decisionmakers endowed with preferences, who form expectations, and face particular constraints. The idea of the economic agent incorporates persons, firms, and other entities such as nonprofit organizations and governments. The essential characteristic of an economic agent is not its physical form but rather its status as a decisionmaker. An agent as a decisionmaker carries within it a straightforward answer to the question of how agents interact. Agents interact through their chosen actions. An action chosen by one agent may affect the actions of other agents through three channels: constraints, expectations, and preferences.

In this book we argue that, it is the strategic behavior of economic agents which can lead an economy to either a high or low level equilibrium, where a low-level equilibrium is a situation where economic performance is low on most relevant counts (GDP per capita, Human Capital, R&D, Innovation, etc.). A poverty trap is a low-level equilibrium defined as any self-reinforcing mechanism which causes poverty to persist (see Azariadis and Stachurski, 2005), and in which economic agents suffer from persistent underdevelopment.

So, the aim of this book is to develop an evolutionary model applying evolutionary game theory to the notion of poverty traps. We study the evolution of the social norm of being either a high-type or low-type in a dynamic environment, where agents are driven by imitative behavior. History matters because given initial conditions, agents imitate according to their current success in payoffs and the current profile of economic agents in the economy. We define a poverty trap as an evolutionarily stable strategic profile and steady state of the replicator dynamics. In this vein, Sanchez Carrera (2012) shows that in poor economies with a large fraction of low-type agents, imitative strategies do not support a take-off into sustained growth. To achieve this take-off, the society should subsidize the critical parameters of the expected payoffs, such that economic agents may change the initial conditions and the economy receives a critical mass of high-type economic agents, so as to overcome the poverty trap.

The number of papers applying game theory to biological problems are in the thousands, since integrated bioeconomic models combining both biological processes (e.g. plant growth, soil nutrient flows, livestock production, agroforestry) and human behavior (i.e. imitative behavior) are increasingly found to be quite useful both as decision support tools and for ex-ante assessment of the performance of new technologies and policies. Although biology clearly supports the conjecture of complementarities (even gens, bacteria, organelles and viruses can be engaged in games of cooperation and conflict), there does not appear to be any formal estimation of the gains from imitative behavior (see Nowak and Sigmund 2004). So what we learn from biological games to economics comes from an evolutionary analysis of an economy where there are both strategic interactions and population structures. This conceptually simple game offers only two strategies (either a type) and four outcomes (either coordinated or not). These prospective general equilibrium effects underscore the importance of an improved understanding of evolutionary poverty traps in systems characterized by imitative economic agents, incomplete markets and non-constant returns to productive assets due to their underlying biology. How to break out of relief traps is indeed a key issue facing many countries today.

Here, we develop a model of poverty traps by using evolutionary game theory. The evolutionarily stable strategy (ESS) developed by biologist John Maynard Smith is the most widely used solution concept in evolutionary games. An incumbent strategy x is played within a population that is susceptible to invasion by a mutant strategy y. Individuals within a large population are paired randomly to play the game. Payoffs are given in terms of reproductive fitness.[1] Although evolutionary stability is the best known concept in evolutionary game theory, it is a static concept that is unable to describe the dynamics of behavioral systems. So studying the replicator dynamics of a system is an increasingly utilized tool for understanding the evolution, for example, of institutions and social norms, providing many applications in development economics (see Gintis 2009). Hence, the aim of this paper is to use the replicator dynamics to study the evolutionary stability of poverty traps, since analyzing the replicator

[1]When we talk of an ESS, we usually model strategies as phenotypes, where it is not trial and error, but an agent programmed with a given strategy, and then it is the survival of the fittest.

dynamics of a system allows one to understand the increasing and decreasing propensity of different behaviors as they meet within a population, leading an economy either to a high-level equilibrium or a low level poverty trap. The equilibrium concept used in the replicator dynamics framework is loosely called dynamic stability, often referred to more specifically as asymptotic stability (Weibull 1995). Intuitively, the state of a population playing a given mixed or pure strategy x is dynamically stable if any small change in the strategy mix does not lead the dynamics away from returning back to x. The following relationships between dynamic stability, evolutionarily stable strategies, and Nash equilibria hold for a general class of games: Every dynamically stable point is Nash equilibrium, but not every Nash equilibrium is dynamically stable. Moreover, every ESS is dynamically stable, but not all dynamically stable population states are ESSs. Thus the ESS is the most stringent of the three concepts, dynamic stability is the second, and the Nash equilibrium is the third.

The model presented here explains how imitative behavior as a culture of cooperation must attain an economic outcome which can lead to a time-stable distribution of economic agents that leads the economy into a social poverty trap. By this, we mean a situation in which the process of cultural transmission between types of economic agents may lead to different long-run levels of equilibria due to certain initial conditions. So we show that a poverty trap is an evolutionarily stable strategic profile of economic agents.

This paper draws from related literature: models of poverty traps and multiple equilibria, and literature on evolutionary game theory and cultural transmission in repeated interactions. This paper relates to several literatures in economics. First, in spirit, the model presented here is similar to that of Accinelli and Carrera (2012). In their article, Accinelli and Carrera develop a model in which several equilibria of economic agents' types can arise. Investment in education can help reach a higher level equilibrium, and therefore transmit more assets to the next generation. However, because of imperfect information, and because the cost of education is indivisible, poor individuals do not invest in human capital, and therefore leave bequests too low for the young to invest in education, i.e. by imitative behavior, they decide to not invest in education. Poor individuals are therefore stuck in the low equilibrium of unskilled jobs (see the seminal paper by Nelson and Phelps 1966; Schultz 1975). More recent studies develop different models to prove that high-skilled labor and high-technological firms are complements in order to obtain a high-level equilibrium (particularly, see Acemoglu 1997, 1998). Acemoglu (1997) considers the same type of interdependence under heterogeneous individuals' human capital. Acemoglu (1998) focuses on skill-biased technological progress and inequality growth between and within groups of skilled and unskilled workers, paying particular attention to common situations in which workers accumulate general skills to prepare for the obsolescence of their technology (firm-)specific skills due to technological progress.

Second, significant articles in game theory have been devoted to the possibility of sustaining cooperation in repeated games (these results are usually referred to as Folk Theorems). Folk Theorems essentially mean that patient players have the potential to sustain higher equilibrium payoffs than impatient players. This is the line, for instance, adopted by Poulsen and Svendsen (2005), who model social capital as the ability to cooperate in a one-shot prisoner's dilemma game. They focus on the possible emergence of a unified norm of cooperation. We instead focus on the possibility of the emergence of heterogenous time-preferences. Contrary to Krusell and Smith (1998) and Doepke and Zilibotti (2008), this paper focusses on the ability to imitate and cooperate as the main channel through which patience affects economic outcome.

More closely related is the literature on learning and adaptive dynamics in games (see Maynard Smith 1982; Maynard Smith and Price 1973, for the early seminal works in this area). One branch of this literature (for example, Young 1993, 2001; Kandori, Mailath and Rob 1993; Binmore and Samuelson 1997) investigates stable patterns of behavior as limit points of various adaptive dynamics. Following the literature on cooperation in repeated games, we model the ability of a high or low type of individual to cooperate by strategic complementarities. In a context of complementarities, cooperation might be beneficial and would therefore help to reach a higher economic outcome from the relationship. But, also, cooperation by strategic complementarities can be risky when the initial conditions are such that adopting the lowest type is the best action, and so the economy can be caught in a low-level equilibrium. These considerations are studied in the present book.

Steven Durlauf has enriched the modeling of poverty traps by adding a spatial dimension: the idea that an agent's socioeconomic outcomes depend upon the composition of the various groups of which she is a member over the course of her life. That is, the decision for an agent to acquire an education strongly depends on the prior existence of other educated members in a group. This interdependence of behavior induces "neighborhood effects", which generate different types of groups that have different steady states (with/without educated members). This interdependence may be intertemporal, i.e. it affects future social interactions.[2] It is this concept of neighborhood effects that, for Durlauf, allows for the understanding of why poverty traps exist and persist. Hence, poverty traps are defined as a community of economic agents that are composed initially of poor members with low-profiles that remain in the low-level equilibrium over generations (Durlauf, 2003).

Poverty traps can therefore arise across geographical locations, and within dispersed collections of agents affiliated by cultural facts and institutions. Group outcomes are then summed up progressively from the level of the agent.

In this vein, Samuel Bowles has built the seminal concept of 'institutional poverty traps', which emphasizes that coordination failures and poverty traps are induced by the presence of specific institutions. Bowles defines institutions as conventions in which members of a population typically act in ways that maximize payoffs given the actions taken by others, such that the process supports continued adherence to the conventions (Bowles, 2006:118).

Polterovich (2008) points out that the formation of institutional traps due to the economic agents with low-profiles who conform to specific strategies is one of the main obstacles to improving economic performance. He defined an institutional trap as a stable yet inefficient equilibrium in a system, where agents choose a norm of behavior (an institution) among several options. It is usually implied that multiple equilibria prevail in the system, and that an institutional trap is Pareto dominated. As with any other norm, an institutional trap's stability means that a system absorbing a small external shock will remain in the institutional trap, having perhaps slightly changed its parameters, and will return to the inefficient equilibrium state once the source of destabilizing pressure is removed. Individuals or small groups of people lose if they deviate from an institutional trap. However, the simultaneous adoption by all agents of an alternative norm may be Pareto improving. Thus the lack of coordination is the main cause of the institutional trap's stability.[3]

Hence, the types of economic agents and their neighborhoods can explain whether a low-level or high-level equilibrium obtains for an economy. We study the idea of neighborhood effects by considering that economic agents interact with an underlying motivation to imitate others.

---

[2] In Durlauf's (1996) model, they create incentives for wealthier families to segregate themselves into economically homogeneous neighborhoods. The dynamics of these combinations explain persistent income inequality.

[3] An important class of poverty traps is due to coordination failures. Many such models are discussed in Cooper and John (1998) and Hoff (2001).

Since, an economic agent imitates his or her neighbors, given a particular state of the economy comprising different types of agents (high- and low-profile), firms and workers could imitate high-profiles engaging in R&D and human capital activities, because imitation is profitable and because there are strategic complementarities between the types of agents. Barret and Swallow (2006) show that when there are multiple strategies in dynamic equilibrium, it implies that poverty traps may arise. Since choosing a strategy means that one implicitly selects the equilibrium towards which one naturally moves over time, given the state of the system, such a strategy is a steady state of a dynamical system.

Therefore, we intend to study the dynamic complementarities and the evolution of an economy composed of different types of economic agents interacting within the constraints of such complementarities and the economic states that obtain.

We have chosen an evolutionary game theoretical model to analyze the above phenomena. Let us continue, in order to explain the advantage of the chosen approach.

1.1. Learning by Imitation

Blackmore (1999) pointed out not only how effective a form of learning imitation is, but also the sophistication required in order to be able to imitate. To explain why agents imitate, we should think of it as a kind of rational behavior. Rational imitation can be explained as follows. An agent, A, can be said to imitate the behavior of another agent, B, when observation of the behavior of B affects A in such a way that A's subsequent behavior becomes more similar to the observed behavior of B. An agent can be said to act rationally when the agent, when faced with a choice between different courses of actions, chooses the course which is the best with respect to her interests, her beliefs about possible action opportunities, and the effects of these potential action opportunities (for a survey on the notion of imitation, see Sanditov, 2006).

Durlauf (2001) noted that the imitative behavior may be due to:

1) psychological factors, an intrinsic desire to behave like certain others;
2) interdependence in the constraints that agents face, so that the costs of a given behavior depend on whether others do the same, or;
3) interdependence in information transmission, so that the behavior of others alters the information about the effects of such behaviors available to a given agent.

Each of these types of imitative behavior implies that an agent, when assessing alternative behavioral choices, will find a given behavior relatively desirable if others have behaved or are behaving in the same way.

In this thesis, we deal with imitation that results in agents performing a spectrum of tasks "as others do". We assume that occasionally, each agent in a finite population gets an impulse to revise her (pure) strategy choice. If these impulses arrive according to independent, identically distributed (i.i.d.) Poisson processes, then the probability of simultaneous impulses is zero, and the aggregate process is also a Poisson process. Moreover, the intensity of the aggregate process is just the sum of the intensities of the individual processes. If the population is large, then one may approximate the aggregate process by deterministic flows given by the expected values. There are two basic elements common to these models. The first is a specification of the time rate at which agents in the population review their strategy choice. This rate may depend on the current performance of the agent's pure strategy and of other aspects of the current population state. The second element is a specification of the choice probabilities of a reviewing agent. The probability that *i-strategist* will switch to some pure strategy *j* may depend on the current performance of these strategies and other aspects of the current population state.

Björnerstedt and Weibull (1996) studied a number of such models, where those agents who revise may imitate other agents in their player-population, and show that a number of payoff-positive selection dynamics, including the replicator dynamics, may be so derived. In particular, if an agent's revision rate is linearly decreasing in the expected payoff to her strategy (or to the agent's latest payoff realization), then the intensity of each pure strategy's Poisson process will be proportional to its population share, and the proportionality factor will be linearly decreasing in its expected payoff. If every revising agent selects her future strategy by imitating a randomly drawn agent in their own player population, then the resulting flow approximation is again the replicator dynamics.

Theoretical advances to understand imitation have been developed by Vega-Redondo (1997) and Schlag (1998, 1999).[4] These two previously

---

[4]Schlag (1998) analyses the imitation rules that an agent should choose, when she occasionally has the opportunity to imitate another agent in the same set of types of players – which I refer to as a player-position – but is otherwise constrained by severe restrictions on information and memory. Schlag finds that if an agent wants a learning rule that leads to non-decreasing expected payoffs over time in all stationary environments, then the agent should (i) always imitate (not experiment) when changing strategy, (ii) never imitate an agent whose payoff realization was

cited works point out how an agent who faces repeated choice problems will imitate others who obtained high payoffs. Despite their basic similarities, these two models differ along at least two dimensions: 1) the informational structure (whom agents imitate) and, 2) the behavioral rule (how agents imitate). While agents in Vega-Redondo's model observe their immediate competitors, in Schlag's model, agents observe others who are just like them, but play in different groups against different opponents. Additionally, agents in Vega-Redondo's model copy the most successful action of the previous period whenever they can. In contrast, Schlag's agents only imitate in a probabilistic fashion and the probability with which they imitate is proportional to the observed difference in payoffs between their own and the most successful action. Apesteguia et al. (2007) show that the different results between the two models occur because of the different informational assumptions rather than the different adjustment rules.

So, whom an agent imitates is more important than how an agent imitates, and in this thesis we confirm this affirmation.

Now, we proceed to explain the notion that we have in mind about high-profile economic agents and the importance of the complementarities between those agents.

1.2. High Profile Economic Agents

The notion of strategic complementarities is widely studied and well understood, and thus the complementarity between R&D (innovative firms) and human capital accumulation (high-skilled workers) is widely accepted as an engine of economic growth (see the seminal paper by Lucas, 1988, or Mankiw et al., 1992; Stockey, 1991). In this thesis, we therefore label innovative firms and high-skilled workers as "high-profile economic agents" and they are the engine driving towards a high level equilibrium.

Nelson and Phelps (1966) and Schultz (1975) pointed out that the major role of education is to adapt to, and to generate, new technologies; that is, to adapt to technological changes generated by innovative firms. Modeling the idea, Nelson and Phelps (1966) assert that the major role of education is, first, to increase the agent's capacity to innovate, and second, to adapt to new technologies, thereby accelerating technological diffusion through the economy. Therefore, high-profile economic agents lead the

---

worse than her own, and (iii) imitate agents whose payoff realizations are better than her own with a probability that is proportional to this payoff difference.

economy to a high-level equilibrium.

Redding (1996) formalizes this idea using an R&D-based growth model developed by Aghion and Howitt (1999). He shows strategic complementarities between investment in education and firms' investment in R&D, and then demonstrates the development trap when both types of investment are inactive. More recent studies develop different models to prove that high-skilled labor and high-technological firms are complements in order to obtain a high-level equilibrium (particularly, see Acemoglu, 1997; 1998). Acemoglu (1997) considers the same type of interdependence under heterogeneous individuals' human capital. Acemoglu (1998) focuses on skill-biased technological progress and inequality growth between and within groups of skilled and unskilled workers, focusing on common situations in which workers accumulate general skills to prepare for the obsolescence of their technology (firm-) specific skills due to technological progress.

In fact, it is generally thought that new technologies reduce the demand for low-skilled workers and increase the demand for high-skilled workers, since high-skilled workers adapt more easily to technological change.[5] This is the well-known notion of "Skill-Biased Technical Change" which implies a shift in the production technology that favors high-skilled over low-skilled labor by increasing its relative productivity and, therefore, its relative demand (see Acemoglu, 2002; Aghion, 2006; Hornstein et al., 2005).

Following this, a number of recent contributors have emphasized the role of skill resources as a crucial constraint on the selection of the technological profile to be implemented in an underdeveloped economy. Hendricks (2000) develops a model of growth through technology adoption focusing on the complementariness between technologies and skills. The workers' skills and the technological profile of firms are complementary because the level of available skills limits the profile of technologies that firms can use, while the technological profile determines the rate of learning. By focusing on the role of human capital in economic development, Benhabib and Spiegel (1994) suggest that the specific role of the human is to facilitate the adoption of technology from abroad and to create domestic technology. This evidence reinforces the importance of the matching between skills and technological profiles. In this sense, Lavezzi (2006) focused on the dynamics of human capital accumulation (by means of a Markov chain) where human capital accumulation and technology

[5]This assumption is akin to the Nelson and Phelps' (1966) argument that greater skills allow for faster adoption of technology.

adoption are interrelated processes. According to him, matching is fundamental in order to isolate one of the most important aspects of the acquisition of human capital and technology. For workers, the crucial issue is the type of firms they interact with, while for firms, it is the type of workers they hire. In the high-skill equilibrium, for example, workers expect firms to invest in technology and then invest in human capital. Given these workers' expectations, firms find it optimal to invest, and therefore expectations are fulfilled in equilibrium.

Some empirical research for Latin American countries (LAC) has been conducted by Cimoli et al. (2009), who point out that the accumulation of human capacities, technological capabilities and the specialization of the production structure shape the response and the way to overcome low level equilibria in LAC. For instance, the Latin American evidence shows a mismatch between the complementarities of innovation and human capital, e.g. the case of the so-called *maquiladoras* in the north of Mexico and low-skilled workers (see Kopinak, 1995),[6] where Mexican labor is inexpensive, and, courtesy of NAFTA (the North American Free Trade Agreement), taxes and custom fees are almost nonexistent, which benefit the profits of corporations. The 'maquiladorized' industry paid lower wages, was non-union in orientation, classified most workers as low-skilled, and was characterized by a high proportion of women workers. An article in *Ward's Automotive Reports* (1997) indicates that the technology mix in Mexican automotive assembly plants is different to that in U.S. assembly plants to take advantage of lower labor costs in Mexico. These lower labor costs reflect the lower productivity of Mexican workers, which itself reflects (presumably) lower levels of human capital. Hence, the type of automotive plant chosen depends, to an important extent, on the skill composition of the workforce. Presumably, the development or adoption of many technologies reflects the supply of factors complementary to the technology. After all, there is no point in developing a capital good that requires skill levels that exceed those of your workers.

Santiago-Rodriguez and Alcorta (2006) investigate the role of human resource management and development practices underpinning firms' performance and innovation in Mexico. The authors critically addressed some of the main challenges and attributes that one may need to take into account to design and eventually implement a study about the nature of links between human resource management practices and firms' performance in innovation.

[6] *Maquiladoras* are export assembly plants in northern Mexico, producing parts and products for the United States.

In a similar vein, Maloney and Perry (2005) studied the LAC and the high tech miracles have followed very different recipes for R&D, FDI, licensing, and education. They show that Latin America has followed a recipe that has relied little on R&D or licensing and too heavily on FDI. This is perhaps a worrying finding given the low rates of technological transfer with FDI, and it appears especially worrying given the generally passive approach to taking advantage of the technological benefits of FDI. In Mexico, for example, despite the presence of IBM and HP, which have been in Guadalajara for 30 years, there is little evidence of a knowledge cluster in computer technologies, at least as captured by patenting data (see Maloney and Perry, 2005).

On the other hand, Argentina and Uruguay are good examples of countries that have accumulated human capital (people with high-levels of education), but with low-levels of advanced technology. Ros (2000) pointed out that Latin American countries are paradigmatic cases of the need for further conditions of a process of sustained growth. Most of them, even with very high initial levels of formal education, did not grow as fast as other countries that started with similar initial levels of human capital.

Further interesting research was conducted by Vonortas (2002) who empirically assessed science, technology, and innovation policy initiatives in Latin American countries. He found that R&D expenditures remain low, with international standards ranging from approximately 1% of GDP for Brazil, to 0.75% for Chile, 0.5% for Mexico, and 0.3% for Argentina. Moreover, their distribution was biased towards governments and universities and against the private sector. Encouraging the private sector to innovate, and particularly the vast majority of small and medium sized enterprises that dominate economic activity, has proven a long and arduous task. Vonortas offers examples from two of the largest and most advanced countries in the region (Brazil and Mexico), a medium-sized, high-growth, relatively advanced country (Chile), a smaller-sized developing country with significant pockets of economic activity (Panama), and three smaller-sized, developing countries (Honduras, Jamaica and Nicaragua).

In any case, in this thesis, we do not want to enter into the debate surrounding, for example, how to conduct R&D, FDI and innovation policy initiatives. The purpose of this thesis is going to be clarified in the next sections, but as we have mentioned, our aim is to study the dynamic complementarities and the evolution of an economy composed of different types of economic agents interacting within the constraints of such complementarities and the economic states that obtain.

1.3. Strategic Behavior of Economic Agents

We argue that the empirical evidence about the mismatch between the complementarities of innovation and human capital can be explained by the strategic behavior of firms and workers, both of which must decide whether or not to invest in R&D and human capital given the current state of the economy. The current state of the economy means the profile or distribution of different types of economic agents, i.e. the current distribution of high and low profile economic agents, which represents the profiles of firms and workers.

The strategic behavior can be explained as follows.

Assume that potential workers imitate their neighbors; that is, they decide to be high or low profile economic agents. Specifically, they decide whether to be a high-skilled worker (e.g, more educated, more able, more experienced) by going to a training school, or to be a low-skilled worker who doesn't incur the costs of training. Such decisions are rational in the sense that they imitate the best performing strategy given the current state of the economy. On the other hand, firms' decisions depend on the composition of labor in the economy. That is, if the number of high-skilled workers is large enough, then a firm decides to be an innovative firm and invests in R&D, otherwise a firm decides to be non-innovative and does not invest in R&D.

Assume that you are a potential worker. First, you need to decide whether to study (say a degree in mathematics or economics or chemistry) or not, and then to enter the labor market and to supply your labor. If you decide to study, then you will be a high-skilled worker, whereas if you decide not to study, you will be a low-skilled worker. The latter scenario currently occurs in most developing countries, where many young people seemingly prefer not to spend more time studying in order to enter the labor market immediately and to offer whatever services they can in order to start receiving a wage, since they observe that a mathematician or chemist or economist is likely to be unemployed. If your decision is taken according to an imitation rule – that is, if you can observe that your neighbors are earning more when they enter the labor market without specializing – then you will imitate them and you will decide not to study. But the converse will happen if you observe that your neighbors are specializing and then are supplying high-skilled labor which gives the maximum expected payoff. In any case, the decisions of potential workers whether to become qualified or not (training or no training) depends on the probability of being hired by innovative and non-innovative firms; that is, it depends on the complementarity between R&D and human capital. At the same time, firms decide to invest in R&D departments just when it is profitable and they base this decision on having a certain number of high-skilled workers to harness new technologies. But if the local economy is highly composed of low-skilled labor, then firms decide not to invest in R&D departments and they may import the necessary technology to produce and to compete.

Hence, we aim to analyze what is likely to occur in developing countries where the population of firms and workers are characterized by a mismatch of high and low profile economic agents, i.e., a mismatch of innovative and non-innovative firms with high-skilled and low-skilled workers.

1.4. Outline

The rest of this book is composed as follows. Chapter 2 summarizes the main notions of evolutionary game theory such as: population games, evolutionarily stable strategies (ESS), the ESS against the field, the replicator dynamics, and the relationships between evolutionarily stable strategies and the steady states of the replicator dynamic system. Moreover, we present the notion of a behavioral rule as a crucial concept of the individuals' behavior.

Chapter 3 studies an evolutionary game of two asymmetric populations where, in each round, a player in population 1 is paired with a member of population 2. We present two imitation models. In the first model, dissatisfaction drives imitation. In the second model, agents imitate the successful. In the first model, we use a simple reviewing rule, while in the second model, we use a proportional imitation rule where switching depends on agents comparing their payoffs to others' payoffs. We show that such imitative behavior can be approximated by a replicator dynamic system. We characterize the evolutionarily stable strategies for a two asymmetric populations normal form game and we show that a mixed strategy is evolutionarily stable if and only if it is a strict Nash equilibrium. In addition, we characterize the evolutionarily stable strategies of our model. Moreover, we extended the model to the application of a specific behavioral rule where a reviewing strategist, *i*, who decides to change her current strategy must consider the probability to imitate a strategy that performs better than her current strategy and the probability of meeting the agent who uses such a strategy. From this investigation, we offer one clear conclusion: whom an agent imitates is more important than how an agent imitates.

Chapter 4 develops an evolutionary coordination game of signaling by economic agents, such that the agents' rational behavior may result in a poverty trap. We argue that poverty traps exist and occur because of strategic complementarities between profiles of agents (for example: low-skilled workers, no innovative firms, and scarcity of human capital and R&D). First, we introduce a coordination game between "leaders" and "followers" with different profiles. Second, we study the game as an evolutionary game of complementarity between the profiles of economic agents. We find the self-confirming equilibria and the ESSs against the field. We conclude that the possibility of either high-level or low-level equilibria implies that economic agents acting under identical settings may experience either an adequate living standard or deprivation (growth or crisis), and this depends only on the initial conditions. Then, if the current state of the economy is composed mainly of low-profile economic agents, the economy converges to a low-level equilibrium since it is rational for every player to imitate those strategists with low-profiles. But if the state of the economy changes and there is a sufficiently high number of high-profile agents, then players imitate those agents with high-profiles, and the economy converges to a high-level equilibrium.

Chapter 5 considers a model where workers' decisions are driven by imitative behavior and firms' decisions depend on the number of high-skilled workers. We analyze the dynamic complementarities between innovative firms and high-skilled workers. We show that when firms invest in R&D in order to become an innovative firm, they are successful only with the presence of a sufficiently high number of high-skilled workers (as in Redding, 1996). At the same time, workers are encouraged to increase their skills when a large number of firms make investments in high technology. Conversely, firms that do not invest in R&D, do not look for high-skilled workers, and therefore make the accumulation of skills unprofitable. We show that there exists a threshold number of innovative firms above which it becomes advantageous to accumulate human capital or high-skilled workers. This is the mechanism that allows an economy to move beyond the poverty trap. Then, we show that if, in a given economy, the percentage of innovative firms is under a certain threshold value, then the economy evolves to a poverty trap where the number of high-skilled workers decreases to zero, and thus it becomes better for firms not to invest in R&D. But we also show that if the initial percentage of innovative firms is higher than the threshold value, then, where workers are following an imitation rule, the economy will evolve to a high level equilibrium. In fact, the high level equilibrium is a steady state of a dynamical system characterized by the fact that a percentage of non-innovative firms coexist with a percentage of innovative firms and a percentage of high-skilled workers coexist with a percentage of low-skilled workers. This result shows the real experience of many developing countries in which there is a mismatch between investment in R&D and Human Capital accumulation, which are the engines of sustained economic growth.

Moreover, the low level (dynamic) equilibrium (the poverty trap) corresponds with a Pareto dominated Nash equilibrium of a two population normal form game, while not one of the possible high level (dynamic) equilibria correspond to the Pareto dominant equilibrium of this game.

Chapter 6 studies the evolution of firms and workers by replicator dynamics. The aim is to extract the evolutionary dynamics from the replicator dynamic system, when the decisions of both firms and workers are driven by imitation. Moreover, we consider payoff taxations and subsidies to achieve the replicator dynamic system where the *target population state* has overcome the poverty trap.

Hence, we characterize the steady states, the ESSs, and the threshold values required to move from low level to high level equilibrium.

We conclude that the imitative behavior of the economic agents can explain the evolution of the economy toward high or low equilibria. Then, if being a high-profile economic agent is the successful strategy because the current state of the economy encourages you to raise your profiles, then imitation facilitates the choice of education (or human capital accumulation), and firms in turn decide to invest in R&D. The crucial parameters that encourage agents to become high-profile are education costs (training costs), skill premia and income tax as a policy to incentivize investment in R&D.

CHAPTER TWO

EVOLUTIONARY GAMES

Before we start with this chapter, let me recommend to the readers the following books on Evolutionary Game Theory: Gintis (2009), Hofbauer & Sigmund (2002), Vega-Redondo (1996) and Weibull (1995).

Now, as we know noncooperative game theory has become a standard tool in modelling conflict between rational agents, where the Nash equilibrium is the cornerstone in predicting the outcome of the game (for refinements on the notion of the Nash equilibrium, see Van Damme (1991)). In a Nash equilibrium, each player's strategy maximizes her payoff, given the strategies played by the other players. No player, therefore, has an incentive to deviate from the Nash outcome, since it is the best situation for each player and for the group itself. But in many situations, it appears that the Nash equilibrium is not unique, though it is certainly very desirable to have the knowledge of uniqueness of an equilibrium, a priori, before actually computing and completing a search. Since there may be multiple equilibria, we may have problems of equilibrium selection, notwithstanding, in which we may not know the dynamics by which specific equilibria are reached because the Nash equilibrium concept is essentially static.

We also face the question of what to do when there are multiple equilibria, with particular attention devoted to characterizing properties that might help to distinguish the equilibria worthy of our attention from less interesting equilibria. The possibility that different refinements will choose different equilibria is only one of the difficulties facing the refinements program.

However, the constant in conventional game theory, including equilibrium refinements and the equilibrium selection literature, is the belief that players are rational, and that this rationality is common knowledge. The common knowledge of rationality is often informally regarded as a necessary condition for there to be any hope that equilibrium will appear. Roughly speaking, the problems upon which an equilibrium refinement is built are often introduced with an appeal to the possibility that players might make mistakes, or that one can only understand "complete rationality as a limiting case of incomplete rationality (Selten, 1975:35)." Thus, the resulting problems typically affect the rules of the game (as in Selten's trembling hand perfection), the preferences of the players and the beliefs of the players. The common practice is to ask a player to stubbornly persists in the belief that her opponent is rational, even after observing a tremble that would provide good evidence to the contrary, if trembles really represented departures from rationality.

A seminal refinement of the Nash equilibrium concept is the notion of an Evolutionarily Stable Strategy (ESS). An ESS is stable against mutants and is asymptotically stable with respect to the replicator dynamics. This latter result shows that rational behavior is not necessary in order to obtain such a sophisticated equilibrium. A population of players who have inherited the behavior of their parents is able to reach an ESS when the offspring are determined by the fitness of the players.

This brings us to the question of what can be learned from evolutionary game theory in studying the evolution of populations and the individual behavior of its members. Evolutionary games consider: i) a selection process that favors some varieties over others, and ii) a process that creates this variety, called the mutation process. In evolutionary game theory, the varieties in question are strategies in a game. In nature, the basic selection mechanism is biological survival and reproduction, and the mutation process is basically genetic. In the market place, the basic selection mechanism is economic survival, and the mutation process is experimentation, externalities and mistakes. In both cases, there is also an element of individual and social learning.

The book, *Evolution and the Theory of Games*, by Maynard Smith (1982) explicitly introduced evolutionary selection pressure in a game theoretic setting. The notion of the evolution of strategies in a repeatedly played game closely resembles certain models in which players learn from past behavior, thus facilitating the shift of attention in the field towards evolutionary models.

Hence, the point of departure for an evolutionary model is the belief that people are not always rational. Rather than springing into life as the result of a perfectly rational reasoning process in which each player, armed with the common knowledge of perfect rationality, solves the game, evolutionary games strategies emerge from a trial-and-error learning process in which players find that some strategies perform better than others, after which they decide to adopt or simply imitate such strategies. The agents may do very little reasoning in the course of this learning process. Instead, they simply take actions, sometimes with great contemplation and sometimes with no thought at all. Their behavior is driven by rules of thumb, social norms, conventions, analogies to similar situations, or by other possibly more complex systems for converting stimuli into actions. In adopting this approach, evolutionary game theory assumes that the behavior driving the process by which agents adjust their strategies may not be perfectly rational, even though it may lead to "rational" equilibrium behavior.

2.1. Strategic Game

We proceed to describe a population game, but to do so we must first recall the notion of a strategic or normal form game.

Let $I = \{1,2,...N\}$ be a set of players; for each player $i \in I$, let S_i be the (finite) set of allowable actions, called the action set.

The deterministic choice of an action $s_i \in S_i$ by player $i \in I$ is called **a pure strategy** for *i*.

A vector $s = (s_1,...,s_n) \in \times_{i\in I} S_i$, where $s_i \in S_i$ is the pure strategy adopted by player $i \in I$, is called **a pure strategy profile** or a configuration of the players. The space of all the pure strategy profiles in the game is thus the Cartesian product $S = \times_{i\in I} S_i$ of the players' action sets (usually called the configuration space).

For any configuration $s \in S$ and any player $i \in I$, let $\pi_i(s)$ be a real number indicating the payoff to player i upon the adoption of this configuration by all the players of the game, i.e. $\pi_i : S \to \mathrm{R}$ defines the payoff function for each player. The finite collection of the real numbers $\{\pi_i(s):\ s \in S\}$ defines **player *i*'s payoff function**. Let $\pi(s) = (\pi_i(s))_{i\in I}$ be the vector function of all the players' payoffs.

Thus, *a **strategic game** is described by a triplet* $\Gamma = (I, S, \pi)$ *where* I *is the set of players,* S *is their configuration space and* π *is the vector function of all the players' payoffs.*

A **mixed strategy** for player $i \in I$ is a probability distribution (as opposed to a deterministic choice that is indicated by a pure strategy) over her action set S_i. We may represent any mixed strategy as a vector:

$$x_i = (x_i(s_i,1), x_i(s_i,2),..., x_i(s_i,m_i)),$$

where $m_i = |S_i|$, $\forall j \in [m_i]$, $s_{i,j} \in S_i$ is the jth allowable action for player i, and $x_i(s_{i,j})$ is the probability that action $s_{i,j}$ is adopted by player *i*. To simplify the notation, we shall represent this vector as

$x_i = (x_{i,1}, x_{i,2}, ..., x_{i,m_i})$. Of course, $\forall i \in I$, $\sum_{j \in [m_i]} x_{i,j} = 1$ and $\forall j \in [m_i]$, $x_{i,j} \in [0,1]$. Since for each player *i*, all probabilities are nonnegative and sum up to one, **the mixed strategies set** of player *i* is the set:

$$\Delta_i \equiv \left\{ x_i \in R_{\geq 0}^{m_i} \ : \ \sum_{j \in [m_i]} x_{i,j} = 1 \right\}.$$

The vertices or corners of this simplex are the pure strategies:

$$e_i^1 = (1, 0, ..., 0), ..., e_j = (0, ..., 1, ..., 0), ..., e_i^n = (0, 0, ..., 1).$$

Hence, a pure strategy is a concentrated distribution of probabilities. Pure strategies are then just special or extreme mixed strategies in which the probability of a specific action is equal to one and all other probabilities equal zero.

A **mixed strategies profile** is a vector $X = (X_1, ..., X_n)$ whose components are themselves mixed strategies of the players, i.e., $\forall i \in I$, $X_i \in \Delta_i$. We denote by $\Theta = \times_{i \in I} \Delta_i \subset R^m$ the Cartesian product of mixed strategies sets of all the players, which is called the mixed strategies space of the game, ($m = m_1 + ... + m_n$).

We write (x_i, y_{-i}) for the strategy profile in which player $i \in I$ plays strategy $x_i \in \Delta_i$ and all others according to the profile $y \in \Theta$.

The player's payoff $i \in I$ **associated with the mixed-strategy profile** *x* is given by **the expected payoff,**

$$u_i(x) = \sum_{s \in S} x(s) \pi_i(s),$$

where $x(s) = \prod_{i=1}^{n} x_{is_i}$ is the product of probabilities assigned by each player's *mixed strategy* $x_i \in \Delta_i$ to the pure strategy $s_i \in S$.

The expected payoff $u_i(x)$ is a linear function of each player's mixed strategy. That is, consider that player *j* plays $s_j = k$, which is equivalent to playing the mixed strategy e_j^k , then the payoff of *i* when *j* uses her *k*-th pure strategy is $u_i(e_j^k, x_{-j})$. Hence, for any $x \in \Theta$, we have:

$$u_i(x) = \sum_{k=1}^{n_j} u_i(e_i^k, x_{-i}) x_{ik}.$$

This combined function $u : R^m \to R^n$ defined by $u(x) = (u_1(x), ..., u_n(x))$ is the combined payoff function of the game.

Hence, the game $\Gamma = (I, S, \pi)$ can be extended, by considering mixed strategies and expected payoffs, as $\Upsilon = (I, \Theta, u)$.

2.2. Population Game

Evolutionary game theory considers populations of decision makers, while analysing the player profiles within these populations, instead of single players. We can therefore identify a population game, where *N* large populations strategically interact as an *N*-player form game, where each player has a large population behind him.

Let us consider an "economy" consisting of $N < \infty$ to be different populations. Formally, we can describe our model of the populated economy as a countable set of populations $P = \{1,...,N\}$. Each population is assumed to form a continuum of positive mass, m_i, $1 \le i \le N$. If we look at an arbitrary population, we simply write *i* for this population, and *i* is an index that can vary between 1 and *N*. Each population is endowed with a finite set of pure strategies, which we can identify with the set S_i. Strategic interactions might take place between and within populations.

In a given game Γ, agents from each of the *N* player populations are randomly drawn and matched to play the game in question.

Then, **a strategy profile** $x = (x_1,..., x_k)$ represents:

- The percentage of agents adopting one of the possible *k* strategies, or
- the percentage of times that the typical agent uses each possible strategy.

In biology, this is genetically programmed, and the payoff corresponds to inclusive fitness or the expected number of offspring. But in economics, agents that play a game many times can consciously switch strategies or behavior. Let S_i be a finite set of pure strategies corresponding to a player population $i \in P$. Then,

Definition 1. *A* ***population state or population profile*** *is an element of the* $(n_k - 1)$*-dimensional simplex*[7]

[7]Consider a finite collection of points in Euclidean R^n, given by $\{x_1...x_m\}$. Such a set is affinely independent if $\sum_{i=1}^{m} \lambda_i x_i = 0$ and $\sum_{i=1}^{m} \lambda_i = 0$ imply that $\lambda_i = 0, 1 \le i \le m$. An $(m-1)$-dimensional simplex is the set of all strictly positive convex combinations of an *m* element set of affinely independent points.

$$\Delta(S_i)=\left\{x=(x_1,\ldots,x_k)\in \mathrm{R}^n \ :\ \sum_{i=1}^{k} x_i=1\right\}$$

generated by the pure strategies $\left\{e_i^1,\ldots,e_i^k,\ldots,e_i^n\right\}$ *For all* $i\in\{1,2,\ldots,n\}$ *the component* $x_i\equiv\frac{x_{k_i}}{m_i}$ *is the proportion of* $i-$ *strategists in the player population k, or the frequency with which strategy* e_i^k *is observed in population k. Hence, a population profile is a vector x that gives the probability* $x(s)$ *with which strategy* $s\in S_i$ *is played in a given population.*

In what follows, we assume that the population masses stay constant, so that we do not have to think about possible effects arising from demographic dynamics. Moreover, we will assume that all populations are of the same size, so every agent in every population is drawn with the same probability. Thus, we can concentrate on Definition 1 to discuss population states.

Moreover, from a modelling view point, we distinguish between two types of population games:

1) **Games against the field**. These games have the following characteristics: i) there is no specific opponent for a given agent, and ii) payoffs depend on what everyone in the population is doing.
2) **Pairwise contest game**. Describe situations where a given agent plays against an opponent that has been randomly selected (by nature).

Consider an agent of any given population where the current population state is *x*. The population profile *x* is generated by the agent's strategy σ . If such an agent plays with σ, then, her payoff is denoted by

$$\pi(\sigma,x)=\sum_{s\in S}\sigma(s)\pi(s,x). \tag{2.1}$$

This payoff represents the number of descendents: either through reproduction or imitation. An agent's payoffs therefore determine the process of evolution in a given population.

We are interested in individual behavior that attains payoffs such that there is no better response for the agent. That is, a necessary condition of evolutionary stability is,

---

$\Delta(x_1,\ldots,x_n):=\left\{\sum_{i=1}^{m}\lambda_i x_i \mid \forall i=1,\ldots,m\ :\ \lambda_i ?0\wedge\sum_{i=1}^{m}\lambda_i=1\right\}$, see Border (1985).

$$\sigma^* \in \arg\max_{\sigma \in \Delta} \pi(\sigma, x^*). \tag{2.2}$$

So, at an equilibrium, the strategy adopted by agents must be the best response to the population state that it generates. The stability condition is therefore of great importance.

Consider a population where (initially) all the agents adopt a strategy σ^*. Now suppose that a mutation occurs and a small proportion ε of agents use some other strategy σ. After the mutation occurs, a new population arises, which is denoted by x_ε,

$$x_\varepsilon = ((1-\varepsilon)\sigma^* + \varepsilon\sigma), \tag{2.3}$$

which is called a post-entry population.

A key concept in evolutionary game theory is that of an **evolutionarily stable strategy** (ESS), a concept conceived by Maynard Smith and Price (1973); see also Maynard Smith (1972, 1974). Such a strategy is robust to evolutionary pressures in a specific sense: a population playing such a strategy is uninvadable by any other strategy. Uninvadability is a useful characterization of evolutionary stability, and indeed its original definition is that a strategy σ^* is evolutionarily stable if and only if (a) it is a best response to itself, and (b) it is a better response to all other best responses than they are to themselves. By definition, no alternative best response exists for any player population if the profile in question σ^* happens to be a strict Nash equilibrium, so such profiles should qualify.

Definition 2. ***A strategy,*** σ^****, is an ESS*** *if there exists* $\bar{\varepsilon}$ *such that, for every* $0 < \varepsilon < \bar{\varepsilon}$ *and every* $\sigma \neq \sigma^*$*, then,*

$$\pi(\sigma^*, x_\varepsilon) > \pi(\sigma, x_\varepsilon). \tag{2.4}$$

In other words σ^* is an ESS if a mutant that adopts any other strategy σ produces fewer offspring in the post-entry population, provided that the population of mutants is sufficiently small.

Evolutionary forces select against mutation if and only if $\pi(\sigma^*, x_\varepsilon) > \pi(\sigma, x_\varepsilon)$; the post-entry payoff is lower than that of the incumbent strategy.

A pairwise contest game describes a situation in which a given agent plays against an opponent that is randomly selected from the population and for which the payoffs depend solely on what both agents do. Then,

$$\pi(\sigma,x)=\sum_{s\in S}\sum_{s'\in S'}\sigma(s)x(s')\pi(s,s'). \quad (2.5)$$

Consider n genetically defined possible behaviors, i.e. there are n-pure strategies, $S=(s_1,...,s_n)$ for each agent in the population. We say that the behavior of the agents generates the profile or state of the population, in the sense that:

- all agents have a mixed behavior $\sigma=(x_1,x_2,...,x_n)$, or
- a proportion x_i of the agents in the population follow the behavior s_i, i.e. they are $i-$strategists.

Consider a population following σ^*. We are interested in knowing the payoff given by $\pi(\sigma,\sigma^*)$.

For the characteristics of the current game, our interest is in the symmetric Nash equilibrium. Recall that every symmetric two player game has a symmetric Nash equilibrium (σ^*,σ^*). We represent this kind of equilibrium by Δ^{NE}.

Suppose, then, that agents initially play according to a mixed strategy σ^* (or that σ^* represents the proportion of agents playing each pure strategy), so in both cases: $\sigma^*=x$. Let x^* be a profile generated by a population of agents, all of whom adopt the strategy σ^*, so $x^*=\sigma^*$.

Let us denote the set of ESS, in a pairwise contest game, by:

$$\Delta^{ESS}:=\{\sigma^*\in\Delta\ :\ (\sigma^*,\sigma^*)\in\Delta^{NE}\} \quad (2.6)$$

The following proposition characterizes the set of ESS in a pairwise contest game.

Definition 3. *A strategy σ^* is ESS, if and only if $\forall\ \sigma\neq\sigma^*$ either:*

1) $\pi(\sigma^*,\sigma^*)>\pi(\sigma,\sigma^*)$, *or*

2) $\pi(\sigma^*,\sigma^*)=\pi(\sigma,\sigma^*)$ *and* $\pi(\sigma^*,\sigma)>\pi(\sigma,\sigma)$.

Corollary 1. *In a pairwise contest population (symmetric) game,*

$$\Delta^{ESS} := \{x \in \Delta^{NE} \ : \ \pi(y,y) < \pi(x,y) \ \forall \ y \in \beta(x), y \neq x\} \qquad (2.7)$$

where $\beta(x)$ is the combined correspondence of best response.

Hence, the concept of ESS is a refinement of NE, because if $\sigma^* \in \Delta^{ESS}$, then:

1) $\sigma^* \in \Delta^{NE}$ and
2) if $\pi(\sigma,\sigma^*) = \pi(\sigma^*,\sigma^*)$ then $\pi(\sigma^*,\sigma) > \pi(\sigma,\sigma)$ (the stability condition).

The following corollary holds:

Corollary 2. *If (x,x) is a strict NE, then (x,x) is ESS.*

2.3 On the Notion of ESS in Asymmetric Games

In this book, we focus on asymmetric games and our baseline model studied in Chapter 3 offers a model of imitation in two asymmetric populations, where we characterize imitation using the ESS concept and Nash equilibrium for such classes of games. Asymmetric games are more realistic in economics because economic agents play different roles such as residents and migrants (or firms and workers), and customarily, there are differences in the structures and methods of competition (see Sanchez Carrera, 2012).

One way to characterize the ESS in asymmetric games is to define a homogeneous set of players who in each period are paired randomly; one of the pair being randomly assigned as player 1, and the other as player 2. We may call this the symmetric version of the asymmetric game. However, an ESS in the symmetric version of an asymmetric game must be a strict Nash equilibrium; that is, each type in the asymmetric game must use exactly one pure strategy (see Selten, 1980, and more details in Gintis, 2009).

Therefore, to apply the ESS concept to asymmetric games, we now think of agents, when called upon to play the game, being randomly (with equal probabilities) assigned to be either player i or player j. The agents are informed of the role to which they have been assigned and are allowed to condition their choice upon this assignment.

Let us consider two polymorphic populations, $\tau \in \{1,2\}$, and at each period $t \in [0,\infty)$, every member of each population is randomly matched with agents from the other population to play a bilateral finite game.

Formally, the game is described as follows:

1) The strategy spaces of each type are denoted by S^1 and S^2, with respective cardinalities $m_1, m_2 \in \mathrm{N}$. Correspondingly, $\Sigma^1 = \Delta^{m_1 - 1}$ and $\Sigma^2 = \Delta^{m_2 - 1}$ stand for their respective spaces of mixed strategies, with generic elements $\sigma^1 \in \Sigma^1$ and $\sigma^2 \in \Sigma^2$.
   a) The payoff matrices $\Pi^1, \Pi^2 \in \mathrm{R}^{m_1 \times m_2}$, here, $a_{ij} \equiv \pi^1(s_i^1, s_j^2)$ and $b_{ij} \equiv \pi^2(s_i^1, s_j^2)$, stand for the payoffs obtained by a player of type 1 (population 1) and a player of type 2 (population 2), where players of type 1 adopt strategy s_i^1 and players of type 2 adopt strategy s_j^2.
2) Assume that agents adopt only pure strategies, and hence the spaces $\Delta^{m_1 - 1}$ and $\Delta^{m_2 - 1}$ are the set of possible population states, i.e. population profiles specifying the fraction of agents playing each of the different pure strategies. Such population states will be generically denoted by x^1 and x^2, where x_i^τ specifies the fraction of agents of population $\tau = 1, 2$ which adopt strategy $s_i^\tau \in S^\tau$.
3) Under the assumption of random matching, for which we abuse the previous notation, we can denote by $\pi^\tau\left(s_i^\tau, x^{\tau'}\right)$, $\tau, \tau' \in \{1, 2\}$ $\tau \neq \tau'$ the expected payoff of playing strategy s_i^τ for an agent of population τ ; when the strategy profile prevailing in the other population is the continuum, such expected values are also identified with the corresponding average magnitudes.

Before we introduce the notion of ESS, let:

$$\Delta^\tau = \left\{ x \in \mathrm{R}_+^{k^\tau} ; \sum_{i=1}^{k^\tau} x_i = 1 \right\} \text{ for all } \tau \in \{1, 2\}$$

where k^τ is the number of pure strategies (behavior) for the population τ .

Definition 4. *A strategy* $x \in \Delta^{\tau}$ *is an ESS in asymmetric games if and only if:*

$$\pi^{\tau}(x_i, y_{-i}) \geq \pi^{\tau}(z_i, y_{-i}), \;\; \forall\, z \in \Delta^{\tau}$$

and for all $y' \in \Delta^{-\tau}$ *,* $y' \neq y$ *there exists some* $\bar{\varepsilon}_{y'} \in (0,1)$ *, such that for all* $\varepsilon \in (0, \bar{\varepsilon}_{y'})$ *and with* $w_{\varepsilon} = \varepsilon y' + (1-\varepsilon) y$ *,*

$$\pi^{\tau}(x_i, w_{\varepsilon}) > \pi^{\tau}(z_i, w_{\varepsilon}).$$

Intuitively, we say that *x* is an ESS if and only if after a mutation in the population, τ continues to be a best response for the post-entry population w_{ε}.[8] However, an ESS of an asymmetric game must be a strict Nash equilibrium, i.e. both types of players, from each population τ , must be monomorphic in equilibrium, there being only one type of player in each population.

Selten's (1980) result shows that an asymmetric game has no mixed ESS, or every ESS in the asymmetric game is a pure strategy (more details are presented in Gaunersdorfer, Hofbauer and Sigmund, 1991; Nachbar, 1990). Therefore, a strictly mixed Nash equilibrium of asymmetric games is not an evolutionary equilibrium under the replicator dynamic (see Hofbauer and Sigmund, 1998).

Let Γ be a normal-form game with player set composed by individuals that comprise two populations labeled $\tau = \{1,2\}$. Each population splits into different clubs denoted by n_i^{τ}, $i = 1,\ldots,\tau_k$. The split depends on the strategy agents play or the behavior that agents follow. Strategies are in correspondence with the clubs, and individuals belonging to the n_i^{τ} club will be called $n_i -$ strategists. Thus, the set S_{τ} of pure strategies are: $S_{\_} = \{n_1^1,\ldots,n_k^1\}$ and $S_M = \{n_1^2,\ldots,n_k^2\}$. Individuals belong only to one club in each period of time, but but in every period, they can move from one club to another.

For each population τ , we represent the set of mixed-strategy profiles by:

---

[8] Vega-Redondo (1996) defines a strategy $s_i^{\tau *}$ being ESS in asymmetric games if given any other strategy s_i^{τ} , there exists some $\bar{\varepsilon} > 0$ such that if $0 < \varepsilon \leq \bar{\varepsilon}$, $\pi^{\tau}\left(s_i^{\tau *}, (1-\varepsilon)s_i^{\tau *} + \varepsilon s_i^{\tau}\right) > \pi^{\tau}\left(s_i^{\tau}, (1-\varepsilon)s_i^{\tau *} + \varepsilon s_i^{\tau}\right)$

$$\Delta^{\tau} = \left\{ x \in \mathrm{R}^{k_{\tau}} \ : \ \sum_{j=1}^{k_{\tau}} x_j = 1, \ x_j \geq 0, \ j = 1,\dots,n_i \right\} \tag{2.8}$$

Note that, a profile distribution $x = (x_1,\dots,x_{k_{\tau}}) \in \Delta^{\tau}$ can be seen as the individual behavior of a player spending a part of his time, given by x_j, in the n_j – club, hence x represents the population state as the vector of individuals' share belonging to each club $i = 1,\dots,\tau_k \ \ \forall \ \tau \in \{1,2\}$.

The normal form representation for our described game is given by the following matrix payoff:

1/2	y_1	$\cdots$	y_{k_M}
x_1	a_{11}, b_{11}	$\cdots$	a_{1k_M}, b_{1k_M}
$\vdots$	$\vdots$	$\cdots$	$\vdots$
x_{k_R}	$a_{k_R 1}, b_{k_R 1}$	$\cdots$	$a_{k_R k_M}, b_{k_R k_M}$

(2.9)

where a_{ij} denotes the payoff of an *i*-strategist from population 1 facing a *j*-strategist from population 2. Analogously for the entries b_{ij}.

The matching between individuals from different populations is done in a random way. We use the notation:

$$E^1(n_i^1 \mid y) = \sum_{j=1}^{k_M} a_{ij} y_j, \ \forall \, n_i^1 \in S^1$$

to represent the expected payoff of the $i-$strategist who belongs to the n_i-club from population 1, given that the typical (fitness) strategist from the other population follows a mixed strategy *y*; that is to say, the clubs' distribution from the opposite population, 2, is given by *y*.

Analogously, the expected payoff of the *i*-strategist belonging to n_i-club from population *M* is given by:

$$E^2(n_i^2 / x) = \sum_{j=1}^{k_R} b_{ij} x_j, \ \forall n_i^2 \in S^2$$

where the clubs' distribution from the other population, 1, is given by *x*. Rational individuals follow the strategic profile that maximizes his expected payoff.

We are interested in the evolution and in the stability of both populations playing the game. Then, we analyze if small changes in the individuals' behavior from one population imply changes in the behavior of the individuals from the other population.

Consider the two-population normal form game:

$$\Gamma = \{\tau \in \{1,2\}, \{S^{\tau}\}, \{A = (a_{ij}), B = (b_{ij})\}\}$$

where each population splits into clubs denoted by n_i^{τ} $\forall$ $\tau = \{1,2\}$ and $i = 1,\ldots,\tau_k$. Hence:

- Population 1 is: $\bigcup_{i=1}^{k_1} n_i^1$, and $\forall$ $h \neq j$ $n_h^1 \bigcap n_j^1 = \Theta$.
- Population 2 is: $\bigcup_{i=1}^{k_2} n_i^2$, and $\forall$ $h \neq j$ $n_h^2 \bigcap n_j^2 = \Theta$.

Let $p \in \Delta^{\tau}$ be the profile distribution of individuals' behavior from population 1, in a given period of time t_0, and that at the same time, the profile distribution of individuals' behavior in population 2 is $q \in \Delta^{\tau}$. Assume that in a post-period of time $t_1 > t_0$, a small mutation affects the individuals' behavior from population 2. Hence, the profile distribution from population 2, after the mutation, is denoted by the offspring:

$$q_{\varepsilon} = ((1-\varepsilon)q + \varepsilon\overline{q},$$

which is called the fitness of the post-entry population. Analogously, the profile distribution from population 1 after suffering a small mutation is:

$$p_{\varepsilon} = ((1-\varepsilon)p + \varepsilon\overline{p},$$

and now, we can state the next definition:

Definition 5. *Let $(p^*,q^*) \in \Delta^1 \times \Delta^2$ be a profile of mixed strategies. We say that the profile (p^*,q^*) is an ESS for an asymmetric two-population normal form game, if for each $(\overline{p},\overline{q}) \in \Delta^1 \times \Delta^2$ there exists $\overline{\varepsilon}$ such that:*

$$E^1(p^*/q_{\varepsilon}) > E^1(\overline{p}/q_{\varepsilon}),$$
$$E^2(q^*/p_{\varepsilon}) > E^2(\overline{q}/p_{\varepsilon}),$$

for all $0 < \varepsilon \leq \overline{\varepsilon}$, and $(p_{\varepsilon},q_{\varepsilon}) \in \Delta^1 \times \Delta^2$ being their respective post-entry populations.

Hence, from the above definition, it follows that if (p^*,q^*) is an ESS, then, the next assertions are verified:

1) The profile (p^*, q^*) is a Nash equilibrium.
2) If there exists some $p \in \Delta^1$, such that $E^1(p/q^*) = E^1(p^*/q^*)$, then $E^1(p^*/\overline{q}) > E^1(p/\overline{q})$.
3) If there exists some $q \in \Delta^2$, such that $E^2(q/p^*) = E^2(q^*/p^*)$, then $E^2(q^*/\overline{p}) > E^2(q/\overline{p})$.

So, the behavior of individuals who adopt an *ESS* performance is better than the mutant individuals' behavior given by the post-entry population. Moreover, for each asymmetric two-population game Γ, there exists a corresponding symmetric version Γ^s. Hence, as Gintis (2009:244) pointed out:

> "[I]t makes no sense to say that a mutant meets its own type when the game is asymmetric, so the ESS criterion has no meaning. The obvious way around this problem is to define a homogeneous set of players who in each period are paired randomly, one of the pair being randomly assigned to be player 1, and the other to be player 2."

In this way, Gintis (2009) defines the "symmetric version" of the asymmetric evolutionary game. Selten (1980) shows that an evolutionarily stable strategy in the symmetric version of an asymmetric evolutionary game must be a strict Nash equilibrium. Let us introduce the symmetric (one population) version for the described asymmetric two-population game.

Definition 6. *The asymmetric two-population normal form game* Γ *has a corresponding symmetric one-population game characterized by:*

1. *The big population:* $P = 1 \cup 2$.
2. *Individuals from the big population P face their own population.*
3. *Let* $n_1^1, ..., n_{k_1}^1$, $n_1^2, ..., n_{k_2}^2$ *be the set of pure strategy for* P.
4. *The matrix payoff for the big population P is:*

$$P = \begin{bmatrix} 0 & A \\ B^T & 0 \end{bmatrix}$$

Hence, the numbered list, items 1-4, characterizes the symmetric version Γ^s *of the asymmetric game* Γ.

Then, for each asymmetric two-population game Γ, there exists a corresponding symmetric version as defined by Γ^s. It is worth noting that these two versions are not equivalent in several aspects.[9] The evolutive properties of the ESS and its relationship with the set of Nash equilibria and the stationary states (SS) of the replicator dynamics for the case of symmetric games are well known (see Hofbauer and Sigmund, 2002; Weibull, 1995). Then, with the purpose of analyzing the dynamical properties of the ESS, let us introduce the evolutionary dynamics by replicators.

2.4. The Replicator Dynamics

The replicator dynamics (RD) explicitly model a selection process, specifying how population shares associated with different pure strategies in a game evolve over time. The mathematical formulation of the replicator dynamics is due to Taylor and Jonker (1978). They imagine a large population of agents who are randomly matched over time to play a finite symmetric two-player game, just as in the setting for evolutionary stability. However, here agents only play pure strategies.

Consider a population in which agents, called replicators, use a pre-programmed strategy, and pass this behavior to their descendents.

Let the population state be a point $x = (x_1, \ldots, x_n)$ in the set Δ of mixed-strategy profiles (defined by (2.8)), where each component x_i is a point in the corresponding mixed-strategy simplex Δ_i representing the distribution of agents in population i across the pure strategies available to that type of player. The vector x_i may thus be thought of as the state of player population $i \in I$ at time t, where $x_{ih} \in [0,1]$ is the proportion of agents in population i who are currently programmed to play pure strategy $h \in S_i$.

Hence, a population state is a distribution x over pure strategies. Such a state is mathematically equivalent to a mixed strategy in the game. If the payoffs in the game represent biological fitness, i.e., the number of offspring, and each child inherits its one parent's strategy, then the number of agents using pure strategy i will (in a large population) grow exponentially at a rate that equals the (expected) payoff $\pi(s_i, x)$ to pure strategy i when played against the mixed strategy x that represents the current strategy distribution in the population. It follows that *the growth*

[9] For instance, for expected payoffs not invariant with respect to positive affine transformations, i.e. substracting a sufficiently large constant from all payoffs in the asymmetric game, then the equilibria of the asymmetric game are unchanged; but in the symmetric version, all symmetric strategy combinations become equilibria.

rate of the population share using any pure strategy i equals the difference between the strategy's payoff and the average payoff in the population. The latter is identical to the (expected) payoff $\pi(x,x)$ to mixed strategy x when played against itself. These are the single-population replicator dynamics for symmetric two-player games,

$$\dot{x}_i = [\pi(s_i,x) - \pi(x,x)]x_i. \tag{2.10}$$

In other words, *the proportion of agents using strategy s_i increases (decreases) if its payoff is bigger (smaller) than the average payoff of the population.*

Note that the best pure responses to the current population state x have the highest growth rate in the population, the second-best pure responses have the second-highest growth rate, and so on. Although more successful pure strategies grow faster than less successful ones, the average payoff in the population need not grow over time. The reason for this possibility is that if an agent is replaced by an agent using a better strategy, then the opponents meeting this new agent may receive lower payoffs.

Moreover, the RD defined for a two population model is:

$$\dot{x}_i^\tau(t) = x_i^\tau(t)\left[\pi^\tau\left(s_i^\tau, x^{\tau'}(t)\right) - \sum_{j=1}^{m_\tau} x_j^\tau(t)\pi^\tau\left(s_j^\tau, x^{\tau'}(t)\right)\right], \tag{2.11}$$

for each $i, j = 1, 2, ..., m_\tau$, where populations $\tau, \tau' \in \{1,2\}$, $\tau \neq \tau'$.

A population state $x \in \Delta$ is stationary in the RD if and only if, for each player population i, every pure strategy $s_i^\tau \in S^\tau$ in use earns the same payoff. Hence, $\forall i \in I$, $\tau, \tau' \in \{1,2\}$, $\tau \neq \tau'$, and the common set of stationary states is:

$$\Delta^o := \left\{x \in \Delta \ : \ \pi^\tau\left(s_i^\tau, x^{\tau'}\right) = \pi_i(x)\right\} \tag{2.12}$$

Consequently, all interior stationary states are Nash equilibria, and all Nash equilibria are stationary: $\Delta^o \bigcap \text{int}(\Delta) \subset \Delta^{NE} \subset \Delta^o$.

Definition 7. *A **fixed point or stationary state** of the replicator dynamics is a state satisfying $\dot{x}_i = 0, \quad \forall i$.*

A fixed point describes a population that is no longer evolving. That is, a solution of the dynamical system $x(t) = x^* \quad \forall t$. The following proposition holds:

Proposition 1. *If x^* is an interior fixed point, i.e., $x_i^* > 0 \quad \forall i \in I$ (all strategy is presented in the population) of the replicator dynamics, then, $x^* \in \Delta^{NE}$.*

Proof. Note that if $x^* >> 0$ then $\dot{x} = 0$, if and only if $\pi(s_i, x^*) = \pi(x^*, x^*)$. Hence all pure strategy must earn the same payoff, therefore, (x^*, x^*) is a NE.

Moreover, it is well known that a fixed point of a dynamical system is said to be **asymptotically stable** or an attractor point if any small deviations from this state are eliminated by the dynamics when $t \to \infty$.

An ESS is a static concept, but it can become a dynamic concept by applying the replicator dynamic equation (see Taylor and Jonker, 1978), and it can be verified that if there is an ESS, then it is an attractor point. The converse is not true: an attractor is not necessarily an ESS because locally, the flow on Δ may spiral elliptically towards the attractor, and it is not covered by the notion of ESS due to the linearity required in the definition. The relationship between the replicator dynamic equation and evolutionarily stable strategies is that every ESS is an asymptotically stable point of the replicator dynamic, but asymptotically stable states need not be an ESS. Zeeman (1992) shows the following result:

Theorem. *An ESS is an attractor point of the replicator dynamic, but this does not apply conversely.*

This result is formally proved by Zeeman (1992); it was first proved by Taylor and Jonker (1978) and Hofbauer et al. (1979) under the assumption that the ESS was regular, and it was concluded that the attractor was hyperbolic. Recall that a point is an attractor of the flow on Δ (the $n-$simplex representing populations with different proportions playing the various strategies) if it is the $\omega-$limit of a neighborhood and the $\alpha-$limit of itself only. Its basin of attraction is the open set of points, of which it is the $\omega-$limit. It is hyperbolic if its eigenvalues have negative real part. Moreover, the theorem shows that from the point of view of smooth dynamics, an attractor is a more general notion than an ESS, and a better characterization of the resistance to mutation.

Then, to characterize the ESS as attractor points of the replicator dynamics, and to characterize the high- and low-level equilibria for such games, we may consider the following theorem:

Theorem. *An ESS corresponds to an asymptotically stable fixed point in the replicator dynamics. That is, if σ^* is an ESS, then the population with $\mathbf{x}^* = \boldsymbol{\sigma}^*$ is asymptotically stable.*

Proof. If σ^* is an ESS, then by definition, there exists an $\bar{\varepsilon}$ such that for all $\varepsilon < \bar{\varepsilon}$ $\pi(\sigma^*, \sigma_\varepsilon) > \pi(\sigma, \sigma_\varepsilon)$ $\forall\, \sigma \neq \sigma^*$ where $\sigma_\varepsilon = (1-\varepsilon)\sigma^* + \varepsilon\sigma'$. In particular, this holds for $\sigma = \sigma_\varepsilon$ so $\pi(\sigma^*, \sigma_\varepsilon) > \pi(\sigma_\varepsilon, \sigma_\varepsilon)$. This implies that in the replicator dynamics that we have, for $x^* = \sigma^*$, $x = (1-\varepsilon)x^* + \varepsilon x'$ and all $\varepsilon < \bar{\varepsilon}$, $\pi(\sigma^*, x) > \pi(x, x)$. Now consider the relative entropy function

$$\mathbf{V}(\mathbf{x}) = -\sum_{i=1}^{k} x_i^* \ln\left(\frac{x_i}{x_i^*}\right).$$

Clearly $\mathbf{V}(\mathbf{x}^*) = 0$ and (using Jensen's inequality $\mathbf{E}f(x) \geq f(\mathbf{E}x)$ for any convex function, such as a logarithm)

$$\begin{aligned}
\mathbf{V}(\mathbf{x}) &= -\sum_{i=1}^{k} x_i^* \ln\left(\frac{x_i}{x_i^*}\right) \\
&\geq -\ln\left(\sum_{i=1}^{k} x_i^* \frac{x_i}{x_i^*}\right) \\
&= -\ln\left(\sum_{i=1}^{k} x_i\right) \\
&= -\ln(1) \\
&= 0.
\end{aligned}$$

The time derivative of $\mathbf{V}(\mathbf{x})$ along solution trajectories of the replicator dynamics is

$$\begin{aligned}\frac{d}{dt}\mathbf{V}(\mathbf{x}) &= \sum_{i=1}^{k}\frac{\partial \mathbf{V}}{\partial x_i}\dot{x}_i \\ &= -\sum_{i=1}^{k}\frac{x_i^*}{x_i}\dot{x}_i \\ &= -\sum_{i=1}^{k}\frac{x_i^*}{x_i}\left[\pi(s_i,x)-\pi(x,x)\right]x_i \\ &= -\left[\pi(\sigma^*,x)-\pi(x,x)\right]\end{aligned}$$

If σ^* is an ESS, then we have established above that there is a region near to $\mathbf{x}^*$ where $\left[\pi(\sigma^*,x)-\pi(x,x)\right]>0$ for $\mathbf{x}\neq\mathbf{x}^*$. Hence,

$$\frac{d\mathbf{V}}{dt}<0$$

for population states sufficiently close to the fixed point. $\mathbf{V}(\mathbf{x})$ is therefore a strict Lyapounov function in this region, and the fixed point $\mathbf{x}^*$ is asymptotically stable.

In general, there may be asymptotically stable fixed points in the replicator dynamics which do not correspond to an ESS. If the derivative of the relative entropy function for a fixed point (taken along solution trajectories) is positive, then the fixed point is unstable. If the derivative is zero, then the fixed point is neither asymptotically stable nor unstable: the evolution of the population is periodic around the fixed point.

2.5. Behavioral Rules

Behavioral rules driven by imitation have a long tradition in the literature of evolutionary game theory. One of the best known evolutionary models, the replicator dynamics, describes an evolutionary process which is driven purely by imitation of others.

In any N player game, there are N populations, one population for each type of player, from which we randomly draw agents who are programmed to play some pure strategy which is available to the type of player. Let these agents play the game. As time proceeds, agents in the populations are allowed to change their pure strategy. This is embodied by so-called behavioral rules; such behavioral rules generate a system of differential equations, which describe the evolution of the relative frequency with which some pure strategy occurs in a population.

There is one differential equation for each pure strategy available to a population and every differential equation describes the evolution of the population share that this pure strategy has; that is, the number x_i^τ for all $1 \le \tau \le N$ and $1 \le i \le n_\tau$. For each population τ, we represent the set of mixed-strategy profiles by Δ^τ as in (2.8), where n_τ is the cardinality of the set of pure strategies available for the population $\tau \in [1,...,N]$.

Definition 8. *A behavioral rule is a map from currently aggregate behavior to conditional switch rates. The map is given by two basic elements:*

1. *The time rate $r_i^\tau(x)$ at which agents review their strategy choice. This time rate depends on the performance of the agent's pure strategy and other aspects of the current population state.*[10]
2. *The probability $p_{ij}^\tau(x)$, that a reviewing $i-$strategist will switch to some pure strategy j. The vector of this probability is written as: $p_i^\tau(x) = \left(p_{i1}^1(x),...,p_{ik}^N(x)\right)$, where $p_i^\tau(x) \in \Delta^\tau$. This distribution may depend on the current performance of the strategies and other aspects of the population state.*

In a finite population, one may imagine that the review times of an agent are the arrival time of a Poisson process with arrival time $r_i^\tau(x)$, and that at each such time, the agent selects a pure strategy according to the probability distribution $p_i^\tau(x)$ over the set Δ^τ. Consider that all agents' Poisson processes are independent, the aggregate process in the subpopulation of $i-$strategists is itself a Poisson Process, with arrival rate $x_i^\tau r_i^\tau(x)$. Consider independence of switches across agents, and consider the process of switches from strategy *i* to strategy *j* as a Poisson Process with arrival rate $x_i^\tau r_i^\tau p_{ij}^\tau$. Assuming a continuum of agents, and, by the law of large numbers, we model these aggregate stochastic processes as a deterministic flow:

- The outflow from the $i-$strategists is thus:

$$\sum_{j \ne i} x_i^\tau r_i^\tau(x) p_{ij}^\tau(x).$$

[10]This is the behavioral rule with inertia (see Bjornerstedt and Weibull, 1996; Weibull, 1995 and Schlag, 1998; 1999) that allows an agent to reconsider her action with probability $r \in (0,1)$ each round.

- The inflow to this is:

$$\sum_{j\neq i} x_j^\tau r_j^\tau(x) p_{ji}^\tau(x).$$

With the use of behavioral rules, we can define an evolutionary dynamic as an inflow-outflow model. Rearranging terms, we obtain:

$$\dot{x}_i^\tau = \sum_{j\in K} x_j^\tau r_j^\tau(x) p_{ji}^\tau(x) - \sum_{i\in K} x_i^\tau r_i^\tau(x) p_{ij}^\tau(x). \tag{2.13}$$

This is a dynamic of replication by extending the concept of replicator dynamics defined for the symmetric case in which a population is confronted with itself. Hence, every behavioral rule (Definition 8) can generate an evolutionary dynamic and they take agents' behaviors as the starting point.

A population dynamic (2.13) will be called imitative if there are at least two different strategies and at least one agent following one of these strategies assesses, with a given probability, whether he should change his behavior. The final decision depends on the relationship between the benefits the agent obtains and the benefits obtained by agents following a different strategy.

Certainly, there are some properties that we would like good behavioral rules to share. A good behavioral rule is Lipschitz continuous in payoffs and social states. That is, to guarantee that this system of differential equations (2.13) induces a well defined dynamic on the space $\Delta = \prod_{\tau=1}^{N} \Delta^\tau$, we consider that $r_i^\tau : X \subseteq \Delta^\tau \to [0,1]$ and $p_i^\tau : X \to \Delta^\tau$ are Lipschitz continuous functions, and there is one and only one solution through any initial state $x_0 \in \Delta$, such that a solution trajectory never leaves Δ. One such property can be seen technically, but also reflects a fact emerging from dynamics within large populations. The state space Δ is forward invariant in this dynamics (2.13).

In fact, if agents had perfect information about all of the payoffs yielded by other pure strategies, and if they knew the state of the population perfectly, behavioral adjustments would be much faster, possibly leading to discontinuous switches. But perfect and complete information is rare in large populations, and no central authority exists that can distribute information fast enough or sufficiently far to reach every agent in society. Hence, Lipschitz-continuity reflects an assumption that people have limited knowledge about payoffs and population states, which has some appeal if we look at large populations.

In the next chapter, we look at the replicator dynamic driven by imitative behavior in two asymmetric populations. The behavioral rule is such that players acquire their behavioral response in part by copying the behaviors of those who, in similar situations, they perceive as successful by some standard, or by acting to maximize their payoffs given their beliefs about how others will act. But others influences are also at work, including conformism or dissatisfaction.

CHAPTER THREE

IMITATION IN TWO ASYMMETRIC POPULATIONS

To adopt an asymmetric approach is crucial in economics. Consider the following examples: economic models with incumbents and entrants in oligopolistic markets, social theory where we need to consider the relationships between migrants and residents with non-homogeneous behaviors, or tourism economics where residents and tourists constitute two non-homogeneous populations with different attitudes towards – and perceptions about – tourism development efforts or environmental quality.

Then, let us consider two asymmetric populations where, in each round, an economic agent of population 1 is paired with a member of population 2, and each of them should decide how to behave. Hence, we propose two imitation models:

First, agents follow a pure imitation rule. They adopt the strategy of *the first person they meet on the street*. Thus, agents randomly select another agent from the population and adopt the strategy of that agent. This behavior is driven by dissatisfaction and is encountered in real populations.

Second, agents imitate successful strategies. Agents take account of their limited cognitive capacities and use imperfectly observed local information to update their behaviors. That is, the probability of an agent adopting a certain strategy by reviewing agents to imitate correlates positively with the payoff currently expected by changing to that strategy. Though each agent imperfectly observes local information, successful strategies will tend to spread while unsuccessful strategies will tend to die out.

We show that these behavioral rules result in an adjustment process that can be approximated by a dynamic system that coincides with the replicator dynamics (as in Accinelli, Brida and Sanchez Carrera, 2009). We proceed as follows. Section 3.1 describes the model. Section 3.2 introduces the pure imitation model where each agent implements her own strategy by imitating because of dissatisfaction. Subsection 3.2.1 discusses the properties of dynamic and Nash equilibria. Section 3.3 presents a model on the imitation of successful agents. Section 3.4 characterizes the ESS of our model. Section 3.5 extends the above model with a modified behavioral rule, called the average rule (see Schlag, 1998; 1999, Sanchez Carrera, 2012). Section 3.6 draws some concluding remarks.

3.1. The Model

Let us assume that agents, at a given period of time and in a given territory, comprise two populations: residents, *R*, and migrants, *M*. Each population splits into two clubs.[11] The split depends on the strategy that agents play or the behavior that agents follow.

Suppose that these strategies are: *to cooperate or not with a member of the other population* (*c, nc*). Those who have a cooperative behavior follow an interaction directed toward a common goal which is mutually beneficial or towards a common purpose or benefit, i.e. joint action. Additionally, to cooperate or not is in fact more profitable when the members of each population are coordinated, playing as (*c, c*) or (*nc, nc*), than in any other situation, i.e. strategic complementarities.

Let $x^{\tau} \in R_{+}^{2}$, be the vector $x^{\tau} = (x_{c}^{\tau}, x_{nc}^{\tau}) \quad \forall \tau \in \{R, M\}$, normalized to one, $x_{c}^{\tau} + x_{nc}^{\tau} = 1$, where each entry is the population share of agents in their respective club.

Each period, an *i*-strategist $i \in \{c, nc\}$ from population $\tau \in \{R, M\}$ reviews her strategy with probability $r_{i}^{\tau}(x)$ assessing whether she should change her current strategy, or not, where $x = (x^{M}, x^{R})$. Hence, $r_{i}^{\tau}(x)$ is the time rate at which agents review their behavior (strategy) choice, which depends on the current performance of the agent's behavior and of the other aspects relative to the current population state *x*.

Let $p_{ij}^{\tau}(x)$ be the probability that a reviewing *i*-strategist really changes to some pure strategy $j \neq i$, $\forall j \in \{c, nc\}$. Thus, $r_{i}^{\tau}(x) p_{ij}^{\tau}(x)$ is the probability that an agent changes from the *i*-th to *j*-th club. In the following, $e_{c} = (1,0)$ and $e_{nc} = (0,1)$ will indicate vectors of pure

[11] A club can be defined as a voluntary group deriving mutual benefits from sharing some facts like: production costs, the members' characteristics, or a good characterized by excludable benefits (see Sandler and Tschirhart, 1997). In this thesis, a club is composed of the agents (players) who follow the same type or strategic profile.

strategies, c or nc, independently from population τ.

Thus, the *outflow* from club i in population τ is $q_i^\tau r_i^\tau(x) p_{ij}^\tau(x)$ and the *inflow* is $q_j^\tau r_j^\tau(x) p_{ji}^\tau(x)$, where $q_i^\tau = q^\tau x_i^\tau$ is the number of *i*-strategist agents from population τ, and q^τ represents the whole population τ, hence $q^\tau = q_i^\tau + q_j^\tau$. For any given population τ (assuming that the size of the population τ is constant), by the law of large numbers, we can model these processes as deterministic flows.[12] Rearranging the terms $\forall\ i, j \in \{c, nc\},\ j \neq i,$ and $\tau \in \{R, M\}$ we get:

$$\dot{x}_i^\tau = r_j^\tau(x) p_{ji}^\tau(x) x_j^\tau - r_i^\tau(x) p_{ij}^\tau(x) x_i^\tau. \tag{3.1}$$

System (3.1) represents the interaction between agents with different behaviors, $i \in \{c, nc\}$, from asymmetric populations $\tau \in \{R, M\}$, under a certain environmental state, $x = (x^M, x^R)$. In fact, (3.1) shows the dynamics of polymorphic populations with agents changing their own behavior under imitation pressure. Furthermore, (3.1) allows us to analyze and to characterize the possible steady states of these populations.

Hence, the aim of this model is to capture an evolutionary stable equilibrium in which all members of the two different populations adopt a behavior that is the best one possible, given the behavior of the agent's own population and the characteristic of the other population. This is precisely a Nash equilibrium for our two population-player game.

Let us denote by $\Delta = \{x \in R_+^n : \sum_{i=1}^n x_i = 1\}$ the set of possible distributions over the set of the different behaviors (the share of each behavior), or pure strategies, in a given population.

We represent by x a distribution[13] of probabilities with regard to the

---

[12] Since we consider a finite population, setting the review times of an *i*-strategist constitutes the arrival times of a Poisson proces with arrival rate $r_i^\tau(x)$, and therefore with such arrival times, the strategist adopts a pure strategy *j* according to $p_{ij}^\tau(x)$. Hence, for any strategist, $i \neq j \in \{c, nc\}$ if their choices are statistically independent random variables, the aggregate arrival rate of the Poisson process of agents switching from pure strategy *i* to *j* is $r_i^\tau(x) p_{ij}^\tau(x) x_i^\tau$.

[13] A distribution is a vector $x \in R_+^n$, $x = (x_1, \ldots, x_n)$, where

possible behaviors of the agents on a given population τ . That is, x is the mixed strategy.

Define the real numbers:

$$u^M(x,y)=\sum_{j=1}^{n}\sum_{i=1}^{n}u^M(e_i,y)x_iy_j$$

and

$$u^R(y,x)=\sum_{i=1}^{n}\sum_{j=1}^{n}u^R(e_j,x)x_iy_j$$

where $u^M(e_i,y)$ is the agent's expected payoff from population M following the $i-th$ behavior, given that population R has the distribution y over the set of her own possible behaviors. Analogously for $u^R(e_j,x)$.

Definition 9. *In a two population-player normal form game with* n *different behaviors in each population, a pair of distributions (a mixed strategy profile)* (x,y) *over the sets of different behaviors in each population is a Nash equilibrium if the expected value is* $u^M(x,y)\geq u^M(z,y)$ *for all* $z\in\Delta$ *and* $u^R(y,x)\geq u^R(w,,x)$ *for all* $w\in\Delta$.

Intuitively, the definition means that x is a best response of population-player M when population-player R displays y, and in turn, y is a best response of population-player R, given that player M is displaying x.

3.2. Imitation by Dissatisfaction

We introduce here the first evolutionary model – a simple imitation model. For a model of pure imitation, all reviewing agents adopt the strategy of *the first person that they meet in the street*, picking this person at random from the population (see for instance, Alos-Ferrer and Weidenholzer, 2006; Bjornerstedt and Weibull, 1995 and Schlag, 1998; 1999).

An agent's decision to stick to a strategy/club or to change strategy is a function of the type of agent she encounters in her own population. We consider that:

$x_i\geq 0,\ \sum_{i=1}^{n}x_i,\ \forall\, i=1,\ldots n$ with x_i being the probability that an agent in a given population observes the $i-th$ behavior. That is, the probability that agents play the $i-th$ pure strategy.

(i) An agent's decision depends upon the utility associated with her behavior, i.e. $u^{\tau}(e_i, x^{-\tau})$ where τ is the population to which the agent following the $i-th$ behavior belongs, given the composition of the other population $-\tau$, $(-\tau \neq \tau) \in \{R, M\}$ and the characteristics of populations represented by $x = (x^R, x^M)$. So, the reviewing rate of the $i-$strategies is:

$$r_i^{\tau}(x) = f_i^{\tau}(u^{\tau}(e_i, x^{-\tau}), x). \tag{3.2}$$

The function $f_i^{\tau}(u^{\tau}(e_i, x^{-\tau}), x)$ is the propensity of a member from the $i-$th club to consider switching membership as a function of the expected utility gains as a result of switching. Agents with less successful strategies review their strategy at a higher rate than agents with more successful strategies.

(ii) Having opted for a change, an agent will adopt the strategy followed by the first population-player to be encountered (her neighbor), i.e.:

$p(i \to j / \text{i considers a change to j}) = p_{ij}^{\tau} = x_j^{\tau},\ i, j \in \{c, nc\}$.

Considering *(i)* and *(ii)*, equation (3.1) can be rewritten as:

$$\dot{x}_i^{\tau} = x_j^{\tau} f_j^{\tau}(u^{\tau}(e_j, x^{-\tau}))x_i^{\tau} - x_i^{\tau} f_i^{\tau}(u^{\tau}(e_i, x^{-\tau}))x_j^{\tau}, \tag{3.3}$$

or

$$\dot{x}_i^{\tau} = (1 - x_i^{\tau})x_i^{\tau}\left[f_j^{\tau}(u^{\tau}(e_j, x^{-\tau})) - f_i^{\tau}(u^{\tau}(e_i, x^{-\tau}))\right] \tag{3.4}$$

This is a dynamic system representing the evolution of a two-population and four-club structure (two clubs in each population). It provides a system of four simultaneous equations with four state variables, where each state variable is the population share of the club members. However, given the normalization rule, $x_c^{\tau} + x_{nc}^{\tau} = 1$, for each $\tau = \{R, M\}$, equation (3.5) can be reduced to two equations with two independent state variables. Taking advantage of this property, from now onwards we use variables x_c^R and x_{nc}^M with their respective equations.

To grapple with the problem, let us assume, consistent with Weibull (1995), that f_i^{τ} is population specific, but the same across all its components, independent of club membership. Assume, furthermore, that it is linear in utility levels. Thus, the propensity to switch will be decreasing in the level of the utility, i.e. $\forall\ i \in \{c, nc\}\ \tau \in \{R, M\}$:

$$f_i^\tau(u^\tau(e_i, x^{-\tau})) = \alpha^\tau - \boldsymbol{\beta}^\tau u^\tau(e_i, x^{-\tau}) \in [0,1]$$

with $\alpha^\tau, \beta^\tau \geq 0$ and $\frac{\alpha^\tau}{\beta^\tau} \geq u^\tau\left(e_i, x^{-\tau}\right)$. To get a full linear form, we assume that:

$$u^\tau(e_i, x^{-\tau}) = e_i A^\tau x^{-\tau},$$

In other words, utility is a linear function of both variables, through a population-specific matrix of weights or constant coefficients, $A^\tau \in \mathbf{M}_{2\times 2}$, $(\tau \in \{R, M\})$. This latter assumption implies that utility levels reflect population-specific (and therefore, in principle, different) properties, i.e., broadly speaking, preference structures over their outcomes. This reduces the previous model to a much simpler version:

$$\dot{x}_c^\tau = \boldsymbol{\beta}^\tau x_c^\tau (1 - x_c^\tau)\left[(1,-1) A^\tau x_c^{-\tau}\right] \tag{3.6}$$

or in full:

$$\begin{cases} \dot{x}_c^R = \beta^R x_c^R (1 - x_c^R)(a^R x_c^M + b^R) \\ \\ \dot{x}_c^M = \beta^M x_c^M (1 - x_c^M)(a^M x_c^R + b^M) \end{cases} \tag{3.7}$$

whose coefficients a^M and b^R depend upon the entries of the two population-specific matrices, A^M and A^R. Note that the system (3.7) is merely a replicator dynamics.

3.2.1 Dynamic stability

System (3.7) admits five stationary states or dynamic equilibria, i.e. $(0,0)$, $(0,1)$, $(1,0)$, $(1,1)$ and a positive interior equilibrium $(\bar{x}_c^R, \bar{x}_c^M)$ where

$$\bar{x}_c^R = -\frac{b^R}{a^R}, \quad \bar{x}_c^M = -\frac{b^M}{a^M}.$$

In fact, the interesting case is when $\bar{P} = (\bar{x}_c^R, \bar{x}_c^M)$ is an equilibrium lying in the interior of the square $\mathsf{C} = [0,1] \times [0,1]$, which occurs when:

$$0 < -\frac{b^R}{a^R} < 1 \text{ and } 0 < -\frac{b^M}{a^M} < 1$$

We can proceed to inquire about the stability of the five equilibria. Recall Zeeman's (1992) result that an equilibrium of the replicator dynamics equations is an evolutionary equilibrium (equivalent to the locally asymptotically stable point in dynamic systems), which is an ESS (for more details, see Shone, 2003).

Proposition. *The steady states* (1,1) *and* (0,0) *are asymptotically stable equilibria, while* $(1,0)$ *and* (0,1) *are non-stable nodes and* $(\bar{x}_c^R, \bar{x}_c^M)$ *is a saddle point when the consistent coefficients range is,*

$$\left\{-\frac{1}{2} < \left(b^R, b^M\right) < 0 < \left(a^R, a^M\right)\right\}.$$

Proof. Via analyzing the Jacobean Matrix, *J*, associated to system (3.7), i.e.:

$$J = \begin{bmatrix} \beta^R(1-2x_c^R)(a^R x_c^M + b^R) & \beta^R a^R x_c^R (1-x_c^R) \\ \beta^M a^M x_c^M (1-x_c^M) & \beta^M(1-2x_c^M)(a^M x_c^R + b^M) \end{bmatrix}$$

Such values, of course, depend on the population specific matrices. Recall that equilibria fitting $\det(J) > 0$ and $tr(J) < 0$ are asymptotically stable points of the game. We thus have the following cases:

1) $x_c^R = x_c^M = 1$, the evaluated Jacobian in this case is

$$J = \begin{bmatrix} -\beta^R(a^R + b^R) & 0 \\ 0 & -\beta^M(a^M + b^M) \end{bmatrix}.$$

when $\left(b^R, b^M\right)$ are positive and $\left(a^R, a^M\right)$ are negative numbers. The determinant is:

$$\det(J) = \left(-\beta^R(a^R + b^R)\right)\cdot\left(-\beta^M(a^M + b^M)\right) > 0$$

$$tr(J) = -\beta^R(a^R + b^R) - \beta^M(a^M + b^M) < 0,$$

and then the equilibrium point (1,1) is a stable node. Otherwise, if $\left(b^R, b^M\right)$ are negative and $\left(a^R, a^M\right)$ are positive numbers, then $\det(J) > 0$

and $tr(J) < 0$, and then the equilibrium point $(1,1)$ is asymptotically stable. Therefore, $(1,1)$ is always a stable node.

2) $x_m^R = x_m^M = 0$, the evaluated Jacobian is

$$J = \begin{bmatrix} \beta^R b^R & 0 \\ 0 & \beta^M b^M \end{bmatrix}. \quad (3.8)$$

Note that, if $\left(b^R, b^M\right)$ are positive and $\left(a^R, a^M\right)$ are negative numbers, it implies that

$$\det(J) = \left(\beta^R b^R\right) \cdot \left(\beta^M b^M\right) > 0$$
$$tr(J) = \left(\beta^R b^R\right) + \left(\beta^M b^M\right) > 0,$$

and then this equilibrium point $(0,0)$ is a non-stable node. With $\left(b^R, b^M\right)$ negative and $\left(a^R, a^M\right)$ positive numbers, $\det(J) > 0$ and $tr(J) < 0$. Therefore, the equilibrium point $(0,0)$ is an asymptotically stable.

3) $x_m^R = 1$, $x_m^M = 0$, the evaluated Jacobian is

$$J = \begin{bmatrix} -\beta^R b^R & 0 \\ 0 & \beta^M (a^M + b^M) \end{bmatrix}. \quad (3.9)$$

If $\left(b^R, b^M\right)$ are positive and $\left(a^R, a^M\right)$ are negative numbers, it implies that

$$\det(J) = \left(-\beta^R b^R\right) \cdot \left(\beta^M (a^M + b^M)\right) > 0$$
$$tr(J) = \left(\beta^R b^R\right) + \left(\beta^M b^M\right) < 0,$$

and then the equilibrium point $(1,0)$ is an asymptotically stable node. Otherwise, if $\left(b^R, b^M\right)$ are negative and $\left(a^R, a^M\right)$ are positive numbers, then, $\det(J) > 0$ and $tr(J) > 0$, and therefore the equilibrium point $(1,0)$ is an unstable node, which is consistent with the fact that $(0,0)$ and $(1,1)$ are asymptotically stable nodes.

4) $x_m^R = 0$, $x_m^M = 1$, the evaluated Jacobian is

$$J = \begin{bmatrix} \beta^R(a^R + b^R) & 0 \\ 0 & -\beta^M b^M \end{bmatrix}. \tag{3.10}$$

If $\left(b^R, b^M\right)$ are positive and $\left(a^R, a^M\right)$ are negative numbers, it implies that

$\det(J) = \left(\beta^R(a^R + b^R)\right) \cdot \left(-\beta^M b^M\right) > 0$

$tr(J) = \left(\beta^R(a^R + b^R)\right) + \left(-\beta^M b^M\right) < 0,$

and then the equilibrium point (0,1) is an asymptotically stable node. Otherwise, if $\left(b^R, b^M\right)$ are negative and $\left(a^R, a^M\right)$ are positive numbers, then, $\det(J) > 0$ and $tr(J) > 0$, and then this equilibrium point (0,1) is an unstable node, which is consistent with the fact that (0,0) and (1,1) are asymptotically stable nodes.

5) The interior equilibrium $\bar{x}_m^R = -\frac{b^R}{a^R}$ and $\bar{x}_m^M = -\frac{b^M}{a^M}$. Evaluating this point in the Jacobian yields,

$$J = \begin{bmatrix} \beta^R(1 + 2\frac{b^R}{a^R})(-a^R \frac{b^M}{a^M} + b^R) & -\beta^R b^R (1 + \frac{b^R}{a^R}) \\ -\beta^M b^M (1 + \frac{b^M}{a^M}) & \beta^M (1 + 2\frac{b^M}{a^M})(-a^M \frac{b^R}{a^R} + b^M) \end{bmatrix}. \tag{3.11}$$

If $-\frac{1}{2} < b^R < 0$ and $-\frac{1}{2} < b^M < 0$ and $\left(a^R, a^M\right)$ are positive numbers, then, $\det(J) < 0$. Therefore, this equilibrium point $\left(\bar{x}_c^R, \bar{x}_c^M\right)$ is a saddle point.

These equilibria can be interpreted as follows:

- The trivial equilibrium obtains when none of the residents are inclined to mix with migrants, nor are any migrants inclined to mix with residents: $(0,0)$.
- Another equilibrium obtains in the opposite corner, where the sharing clubs involve all of their respective populations. Here, reciprocal integration of the two populations is complete at (1,1).

  The two remaining border equilibria show a different club dominating the two populations and in a sense constitute a mismatch between strategies: $(0,1)$, $(1,0)$.
- Finally, we have the interior equilibrium. This equilibrium implies

that a certain percentage of each population is well-disposed to the other population, while the rest only accept marriage between members of their own populations: $\overline{P} = (\overline{x}_c^R, \overline{x}_c^M)$.

3.3. Adopting the Most Successful Strategy

The rule now states that an agent must choose an action with the best payoff with a probability proportional to the expected payoff. In other words, a migrant (resident) will change to a strategy played by another member of her population if and only if the alternative strategy brings greater expected utility, i.e. a greater payoff. We assume that every reviewing strategist samples at random from her own population and that she can observe, with some noise, an average payoff of the sampled agent's strategy.

Let us assume that a reviewing strategist, from population $\tau \in \{R, M\}$, with behavior (club) $j \in \{c, nc\}$, meets another agent with an alternative behavior (club) $i \neq j$, and that, she will change from *j* to *i* if and only if:

$$u^\tau(e_i, x^{-\tau}) > u^\tau(e_j, x^{-\tau}). \tag{3.12}$$

The utility of each agent depends on her own strategy and on the characteristics of the agents of the other population. Further, we assume that there is some uncertainty in the strategies' estimated utility, so that each reviewing strategist must estimate the value of $u^\tau(e_i, x^{-\tau})$.

Let $\overline{D}$ be the estimator for the difference $u^\tau(e_i, x^{-\tau}) - u^\tau(e_j, x^{-\tau})$. Let $P^\tau(\overline{D} \geq 0)$ be the probability that the estimated $\overline{D}$ is positive.

In such a way, let p_{ji}^τ be the probability that *j* changes to *i*. This probability is given by

$$p_{ji}^\tau = x_{ji}^\tau P^\tau(\overline{D} \geq 0),$$

where x_{ji}^τ is the probability that *j*-strategist meets an *i*-strategist, $\forall$ $\tau \in \{R, M\}$. Let us assume that $P^\tau(\overline{D} \geq 0)$ depends upon the true value of the difference $u^\tau(e_i, x^{-\tau}) - u^\tau(e_j, x^{-\tau})$ which is unknown to the *i*-th agent. That is

$$P^{\tau}(\bar{D} \geq 0) = \phi^{\tau}\left(u^{\tau}(e_i,x^{-\tau}) - u^{\tau}(e_j,x^{-\tau})\right) \tag{3.13}$$

where $\phi : R \rightarrow [0,1]$ is a differentiable probability distribution. Therefore, the probability that a j-strategist from population τ estimates a positive value $\bar{D}$ increases with the true value of the difference $u^{\tau}(e_j,x^{-\tau}) - u^{\tau}(e_i,x^{-\tau})$. For the sake of simplicity, let $u^{\tau}(e_i,x^{\tau})$ be linear, i.e.,

$$u^{\tau}(e_i,x^{-\tau}) = e_i A^{\tau} x^{-\tau}. \tag{3.14}$$

Thus, from equations (3.13) and (3.14), the probability that a j-strategist changes to the i-th strategy is:

$$p_{ji}^{\tau}(u^{\tau}(e_i - e_j,x^{-\tau})) = \phi^{\tau}(u^{\tau}(e_i - e_j,x^{-\tau}))x_i^{\tau}, \tag{3.15}$$

Hence, the change in the share of the i-strategist will be given by the probability that a j-strategist becomes an i-strategist weighted by the relative number of j-strategists minus the probability that an i becomes a j-strategist, likewise weighted:

$$\dot{x}_i^{\tau} = \left[x_j^{\tau} p_{ji}^{\tau} - p_{ij}^{\tau} x_i^{\tau}\right] x_i^{\tau}.$$

In this case, the equation is:

$$\dot{x}_i^{\tau} = x_j^{\tau} x_i^{\tau}\left[\phi^{\tau}(u^{\tau}(e_j - e_i,x^{-\tau})) - \phi^{\tau}(u^{\tau}(e_i - e_j,x^{-\tau}))\right] \tag{3.16}$$

and a first order approximation is given by:[14]

$$\begin{aligned}\dot{x}_i^{\tau} &= x_i^{\tau} x_j^{\tau}[\tau\phi^{\tau'}(0,)\left[u^{\tau}(e_j - e_i,x^{-\tau}) - u^{\tau}(e_j - e_i,x^{-\tau}))\right] = \\ &= 2\phi^{\tau'}(0)u^{\tau}(e_i - x^{\tau},x^{-\tau})x_i^{\tau}.\end{aligned} \tag{3.17}$$

Hence, in a neighborhood of an interior stationary point, the dynamics are approximately represented by the replicator dynamics multiplied by a constant. Stability analysis of the local type can therefore be carried out

[14]Note that for this dynamic, the set of interior stationary state coincides with the set of interior Nash equilibria.

using the linear part of the nonlinear system.[15] In the special case where ϕ^{τ} is linear, i.e.:

$$\phi^{\tau} = \lambda_{\tau} + \mu^{\tau} u^{\tau}(e_j - e_i, x^{\tau})$$

where λ^{τ} and μ^{τ} verify:

$$0 \le \lambda^{\tau} + \mu^{\tau} u(x^{\tau}, x^{-\tau}) \le 1,\ \forall\, x \in \left\{ z \in R_{+}^{2}\ :\ \max_{i=1,2} z_i \le 1 \right\}.$$

Thus, for each behavior i and each population τ the following equation holds:

$$\dot{x}_i^{\tau} = 2\mu^{\tau} u^{\tau}(e_i - x^{\tau}, x^{-\tau}) x_i^{\tau}, \tag{3.18}$$

which is merely a replicator dynamic.

Hence, stability analysis is similar to the analysis of the model of pure imitation driven by dissatisfaction. Thus, whom an agent imitates is more important than how an agent imitates.

3.4. Evolutionarily Stable Strategies

A strategy is an evolutionarily stable strategy (ESS) if a whole population playing that strategy cannot be invaded by a small group with a mutant genotype. Similarly, a cultural form is an ESS if, upon being adopted by all members of a society (firm, family, etc.), no small group of agents using an alternative cultural form can invade. As Gintis (2009) noted, we move from explaining the actions of agents to modeling the diffusion of forms of behavior (strategies) in society.

We now introduce a definition of ESS in the framework of our model where there are two populations playing an asymmetric normal form game. To introduce this concept in our model, let us consider the following representation: Let $N_{\tau j}$ be the total of j-strategists, $j \in \{c, nc\}$, in population $\tau \in \{M, R\}$, and let $H = N_{Mc} + N_{Mnc} + N_{Rc} + N_{Rnc}$ be the total number of inhabitants in the country. Let us denote by $x_{1R} = \frac{N_{Rc}}{H}$, $x_{2R} = \frac{N_{Rnc}}{H}$, $x_{1M} = \frac{N_{Mc}}{H}$, $x_{2M} = \frac{N_{Mnc}}{H}$. Then, we denote by:

$$\Delta = \left\{ x \in R_{+}^{4}\ :\ x_{1R} + x_{2R} + x_{1M} + x_{2M} = 1 \right\}$$

the $(k-1)$ – simplex of R_k; in our case, $k = 4$. Also, we introduce the

[15] If the equilibrium is non hyperbolic.

symbolism: $x=(x^R,x^M)$ where $x^\tau=(x_{1\tau},x_{2\tau}),\forall\tau\in\{M,R\}$.

Let us now introduce the following notation:

$$\bar{x}_c^R=\frac{H}{|R|}x_{1R},\ \bar{x}_{nc}^R=\frac{H}{|R|}x_{2R},\ \bar{x}_c^M=\frac{H}{|M|}x_{1M},\ \bar{x}_{nc}^M=\frac{H}{|M|}x_{2M}$$

where $|R|$ is the total number of agents in population R, and $|M|$ is the total number of agents in population M, and $\bar{x}^\tau=(\bar{x}_c^\tau,\bar{x}_{nc}^\tau),\ \forall\tau\in\{R,M\}$.

Definition 10. *We say that* $x\in\Delta$ *is an* ***evolutionarily stable strategy (ESS)****, if and only if for every* $y\in\Delta$, $y\neq x$ *there exists some* $\bar{\varepsilon}_y\in(0,1)$ *such that for all* $\varepsilon\in(0,\bar{\varepsilon}_y)$ *and with* $w=\varepsilon y+(1-\varepsilon)x$ *where* $w=(w^R,w^M)=\varepsilon(y^R,y^M)+(1-\varepsilon)(x^R,x^M)$, *then:*

$$u^\tau(\bar{x}^\tau,\bar{w}^{-\tau})>u^\tau(\bar{y}^\tau,\bar{w}^{-\tau}),\ \ \forall\tau\in\{R,M\}.$$

Intuitively, we say that a distribution x is an ESS if the incumbent strategy x^τ does better in the post-entry population than the alternative strategy y^τ, $\forall\tau$. In our definition, agents of a given population do not play against agents in their own population, so the second order conditions in the definition of an ESS become superfluous.

The next theorem shows the equivalence between our definition of ESS in the framework of asymmetric normal form games and the definition of a strict Nash equilibrium.[16]

Theorem. *If the distribution* $x=(x_{1R},x_{2R},x_{1M},x_{2M})$ *is an ESS in the sense of* ***Definition def:ess*** *then, the profile of mixed strategies* $\bar{x}=(\bar{x}^R,\bar{x}^M)=(\bar{x}_c^R,\bar{x}_{nc}^R,\bar{x}_c^M,\bar{x}_{nc}^M)$ *is a strict Nash equilibrium for the two population normal form game and conversely, for each strict Nash equilibrium* $\bar{x}$, *there exists a distribution* x *that is an ESS.*

Proof. Let $S^\tau,\tau\in\{M,R\}$ be the set of mixed strategies of the populations M and R. The theorem follows immediately from our definition of ESS (Definition 10), the definition of strict Nash equilibrium

[16]Recall that a Nash equilibrium $s=(x,y)$ is called strict if and only if the profile s is the unique best reply against itself.

and the continuity of the functions $u_\tau : S^\tau \times S^{-\tau} \to R$. Note that from the definition of ESS it follows that $u_\tau(\bar{x}^\tau, \bar{x}^{-\tau}) > u_\tau(\bar{y}^\tau, \bar{x}^{-\tau})\ \forall\ y^\tau \neq x^\tau \in S^\tau$ and $\forall \tau$ so, $\bar{x}^\tau$ is the only best response against $\bar{x}^{-\tau}$ $\tau \in \{M, R\}$.

Note that a distribution $x \in \Delta$ defines an interior stationary point for each one of the dynamical systems (3.18) if and only if,

$$u^\tau(e_i, \bar{x}^{-\tau}) = u(\bar{x}^\tau, \bar{x}^{-\tau}).$$

This means that x^τ is a best response for population $\tau = \{M, R\}$ against $x^{-\tau}$ so, the profile $(x^\tau, x^{-\tau})$ is a Nash equilibrium. And conversely, if the profile $(x^\tau, x^{-\tau})$ is a Nash equilibrium, then it is a stationary point for these dynamical systems.

Theorem. *If the distribution* $x = (x_{1R}, x_{2R}, x_{1M}, x_{2M})$ *is an ESS* ***(Definition 10)****, then the profile of mixed strategies* $\bar{x} = (\bar{x}^R, \bar{x}^M)$ *is a globally asymptotically stable stationary point of (3.17) or (3.18).*

Proof. Consider the relative entropy function $H_x : Q_x \to R$, where Q_x is the set of the distributions $y \in \Delta$ that assign probability positive to every state that has probability positive in *x*. In fact, Q_x is the union of the interior of the simplex Δ at the minimal boundary face containing *x*. Then:

$$H_x(y) = -\sum_{i \in C(x)} x_i \ln\left(\frac{y_i}{x_i}\right) = -\sum_{i \in C(x^M)} x_i^M \ln\left(\frac{y_i^M}{x_i^M}\right) - \sum_{i \in C(x^R)} x_i^R \ln\left(\frac{y_i^R}{x_i^R}\right)$$

By $C(x)$, we denote the support of *x*, i.e. the set of coordinates not equal to 0. As it is easy to see, if *x* is an ESS, then $H_x(y)$ verifies that:

1) $H_x(y) = 0$ if and only if $y = x$.
2) $\dot{H}_x(y) = -\sum_{i=1}^{4} \dot{y}_i x_i =$
   $= -k\left[\left(u^M(x^M, y^R) - u^M(y^M, y^R)\right) + \left(u^R(x^R, y^M) - u^R(y^R, y^M)\right)\right],$
   where:

$$k = \begin{cases} \beta^{\tau} \text{ if the system is (3.17),} \\ \\ 2\mu^{\tau} \text{ if the system is by (3.18).} \end{cases}$$

Thus, if x is an ESS, then $\dot{H}_x(y) < 0 \; \forall \; y \in U \cap Q_x$ where U is a neighborhood of x. In this context, this theorem make it known that when a population has a distribution that is an ESS, if this composition is perturbed (in a relative neighborhood of x), then the performance of all strategies in this population decreases with respect to the original distribution x.

In other words, if x is an ESS, then not only is the best distribution within each group, given the behavior of the population in the given country, it is also a stable strategy in the sense that every change in the distribution of the behavior within a group implies a worse payoff for the deviating group. Moreover, if x is an ESS and the corresponding $\bar{x}_c = (\bar{x}_c^R, \bar{x}_c^M)$ is an interior stationary point for the dynamical system given by (eqb) or by (eqc), it follows that for every solution $\xi(t, z_0)$ of these systems of equations, with initial conditions z_0 in the interior of the square $[0,1]\times[0,1]$, it is implied that $\xi(t, z_0)_{t\to\infty} \to \bar{z}$. This means that $\bar{z}$ is a globally asymptotically stable stationary point, in the sense of attracting all interior initial states. Hence, if the distribution of the population $x = (x_{1R}, x_{2R}, x_{1M}, x_{2M})$ in $t = t_0$ is perturbed to a new distribution y, then the evolution of this perturbed distribution, whose state, in each time t is denoted by $\phi(t, y)$, where $\phi(t_0, y) = y$, evolves according to one of the dynamical systems (eqb) or (eqc), y will always approach the initial distribution x.

3.5. The Specific Behavioral Rule

An evaluation rule that seems particularly natural in a context of simple imitation is the average rule where each strategy is evaluated according to the average payoff observed in the reference group (see J. Apesteguia et al., 2007).

Let us consider Definition 8 of a Behavioral Rule; but now we define p_{ij}^{τ} as the probability of finding a better performing strategy j and finding or meeting such a better performing agent, x_j^{τ}.

Assume that there is some uncertainty in the strategies' estimated utility, so that each reviewing strategist, $(j \neq i) \in \{c, nc\}$, should estimate their corresponding value of $u^\tau(\cdot)$. Let $\bar{u}^\tau(e_j, \cdot)$ and $\bar{u}^\tau(e_i, \cdot)$ be the estimators of the real values $u^\tau(e_j, \cdot)$ and $u^\tau(e_i, \cdot)$. Then, the specific behavioral rule is:

Definition 11. *A reviewing strategist i changes to j with probability,* p_{ij}^τ, *equal to:*

$$P[\bar{u}^\tau(e_j, \cdot) > \bar{u}^\tau(e_i, \cdot)]x_j^\tau = \begin{cases} \lambda u^\tau(e_j, x^{-\tau})x_j^\tau & \text{if } u^\tau(e_j, x^{-\tau}) > 0 \\ 0 & \text{if } u^\tau(e_j, x^{-\tau}) \le 0 \end{cases} \tag{3.19}$$

where $\lambda = \frac{1}{|u^\tau(e_i, x^{-\tau}) + u^\tau(e_j, x^{-\tau})|}$, $-\tau \neq \tau \in \{R, M\}$ *and* $i \neq j \in \{c, nc\}$.

Therefore, the equations (3.5 and 3.18) can be rewritten as:

$$\dot{x}_i^\tau = f_j^\tau(u^\tau(e_j, x^{-\tau}))\lambda u^\tau(e_i, x^{-\tau})x_i^\tau x_j^\tau - f_i^\tau(u^\tau(e_i, x^{-\tau}))\lambda u^\tau(e_j, x^{-\tau})x_j^\tau x_i^\tau \tag{3.20}$$

To simplify, let us label the functions $u^\tau(e_i, x^{-\tau}) = u_i^\tau$ and $u^\tau(e_j, x^{-\tau}) = u_j^\tau$, then, we can write,

$$\dot{x}_i^\tau = (1 - x_i^\tau)x_i^\tau \lambda \left[f_j^\tau(u_j^\tau)u_i^\tau - f_i^\tau(u_i^\tau)u_j^\tau\right] \tag{3.21}$$

Once again, consider that f_i^τ is population specific; thus, the propensity to switch behavior is decreasing in the level of utility (see Weibull, 1995), i.e.:

$$f_i^\tau(u_i^\tau) = \alpha^\tau - \boldsymbol{\beta}^\tau u_i^\tau, \tag{3.22}$$

with $\alpha^\tau, \beta^\tau \ge 0$, and $\frac{\alpha^\tau}{\beta^\tau} \ge u_i^\tau$ assure that $f_i^\tau(u_i^\tau) \in [0,1]$. Thus, with respect to the utility level of the *i*-strategist, u_i^τ increases her average reviewing rate, and $r_i^\tau(x) = f_i^\tau(u_i^\tau)$ will decrease.

Therefore, considering the above behavioral rule (Definition 11) and equation (3.22), we obtain the system of replicator dynamic equations driven by imitation, i.e.:

$$\dot{x}_i^\tau = \lambda x_i^\tau (1 - x_i^\tau) \left[\alpha^\tau \left(\frac{u_i^\tau - u_j^\tau}{u_i^\tau + u_j^\tau} \right) \right]. \tag{3.23}$$

Or in full:

$$\begin{cases} \dot{x}_c^R = -\dot{x}_{nc}^R = \alpha^R x_c^R (1 - x_c^R) \left(\frac{u_c^R - u_{nc}^R}{u_c^R + u_{nc}^R} \right) \\ \dot{x}_c^M = -\dot{x}_{nc}^M = \alpha^M x_c^M (1 - x_c^M) \left(\frac{u_c^M - u_{nc}^M}{u_c^M + u_{nc}^M} \right) \end{cases} \tag{3.24}$$

System (3.24) describes the replicator dynamic model as a process where only those strategies that are better than the population average can replicate. The system $(\dot{x}_c^R, \dot{x}_c^M)$ admits five stationary states or dynamic equilibria, i.e.:

$$(0,0),\ (0,1),\ (1,0),\ (1,1) \text{ and } \bar{P} = (\bar{x}_c^R, \bar{x}_c^M)$$

where:

$$\bar{x}_c^R = \alpha^R, \quad \bar{x}_c^M = \alpha^M$$

is the mixed-strategy Nash equilibrium. $\bar{P} = (\bar{x}_c^R, \bar{x}_c^M)$ is lying in the interior of the square $\mathsf{C} = [0,1] \times [0,1]$, or $0 < \alpha^R < 1$ and $0 < \alpha^M < 1$.

We should identify all the attractors and saddle points, as well as the basins of attraction. The volume of the space covered by a basin is proportional to the probability that a mixed-Nash equilibrium will be adopted. Thus, basins of attraction provide insights into which equilibria are more likely to be adopted depending on the state.

To study the dynamics, we should have a functional form of $u^\tau(e_i, x^{-\tau}) = u_i^\tau$ and $u^\tau(e_j, x^{-\tau}) = u_j^\tau$. For instance, for all $i \neq j \in \{c, nc\}, -\tau \neq \tau \in \{R, M\}$. We can assume the linear form:

$$u_i^\tau = a^\tau x_i^{-\tau} - \left(1 - a^\tau\right) x_j^{-\tau} + b^\tau,$$

where $a^{\tau} \in [0,1]$ and $b^{\tau} > 0$, with strategic complementarities across populations $\frac{\partial u_i^{\tau}}{\partial x_i^{-\tau}} > 0$ and $\frac{\partial u_j^{\tau}}{\partial x_j^{-\tau}} > 0$. The next proposition summarizes our main result,

Proposition. *The steady states* $(1,1)$ *and* $(0,0)$ *are asymptotically stable equilibria, while* $(1,0)$ *and* $(0,1)$ *are non-stable nodes. The mixed-strategy Nash equilibrium* $\overline{P} = (\overline{x}_c^R, \overline{x}_c^M)$ *is a saddle point, and, with the exception of a single curve through this point, all solution trajectories converge to* $(1,1)$ *or* $(0,0)$.

Proof. The Jacobean associated to the system $\left(\dot{x}_c^R, \dot{x}_c^M\right)$ is,

$$J = \begin{bmatrix} \alpha^R - \left(\frac{u_c^R - u_{nc}^R}{u_c^R + u_{nc}^R}\right) & \alpha^R x_c^R (1 - x_c^R) \cdot \frac{\partial\left(\frac{u_c^R - u_{nc}^R}{u_c^R + u_{nc}^R}\right)}{\partial x_c^M} \\ \alpha^M x_c^M (1 - x_c^M) \cdot \frac{\partial\left(\frac{u_c^M - u_{nc}^M}{u_c^M + u_{nc}^M}\right)}{\partial x_c^R} & \alpha^M - \left(\frac{u_c^M - u_{nc}^M}{u_c^M + u_{nc}^M}\right) \end{bmatrix}$$

Such values, of course, depend on the population specific matrices. Recall that equilibria fitting $\det(J) > 0$ and $tr(J) < 0$ are asymptotically stable for the game.

We evaluate $J\left(\dot{x}_c^R, \dot{x}_c^M\right)$,

1) $x_c^R = x_c^M = 0$. The evaluated Jacobean in this case is given by,

$$J = \begin{bmatrix} \alpha^R - \left(\frac{u_c^R - u_{nc}^R}{u_c^R + u_{nc}^R}\right) & 0 \\ 0 & \alpha^M - \left(\frac{u_c^M - u_{nc}^M}{u_c^M + u_{nc}^M}\right) \end{bmatrix}$$

It yields $\det(J) > 0$ and $tr(J) < 0$. Hence this equilibrium point (0,0) is an attractor and therefore ESS.

2) Similarly, when $x_c^R = x_c^M = 1$, the evaluated Jacobean is,

$$J = \begin{bmatrix} \alpha^R - \left(\frac{u_c^R - u_{nc}^R}{u_c^R + u_{nc}^R} \right) & 0 \\ 0 & \alpha^M - \left(\frac{u_c^M - u_{nc}^M}{u_c^M + u_{nc}^M} \right) \end{bmatrix}$$

and $\det(J) > 0$ and $tr(J) < 0$. Therefore, the cooperation equilibrium (1,1) is asymptotically stable and hence an ESS.

3) The interior equilibrium $\bar{x}_c^R = \alpha^R$ and $\bar{x}_c^M = \alpha^M$. Evaluating this point in the Jacobean yields,

$$J = \begin{bmatrix} \alpha^R - \left(\frac{u_c^R - u_{nc}^R}{u_c^R + u_{nc}^R} \right) & \left(\alpha^R\right)^2 (1 - \alpha^R) \cdot \frac{\partial \left(\frac{u_c^R - u_{nc}^R}{u_c^R + u_{nc}^R} \right)}{\partial x_c^M} \\ \left(\alpha^M\right)^2 (1 - \alpha^M) \cdot \frac{\partial \left(\frac{u_c^M - u_{nc}^M}{u_c^M + u_{nc}^M} \right)}{\partial x_c^R} & \alpha^M - \left(\frac{u_c^M - u_{nc}^M}{u_c^M + u_{nc}^M} \right) \end{bmatrix},$$

by strategic complementarities: $\det(J) < 0$, thus the equilibrium point $\bar{P} = (\bar{x}_c^R, \bar{x}_c^M)$ is a saddle point. Therefore, $\bar{P} = (\bar{x}_c^R, \bar{x}_c^M)$ is a threshold, since, it separates the basins of attraction of the low-level and high-level equilibria.

Figure 3-1 gives a graphic representation of the solution orbits for the standard two-population replicator dynamics $\left(\dot{x}_c^R, \dot{x}_c^M\right)$ driven by imitation.

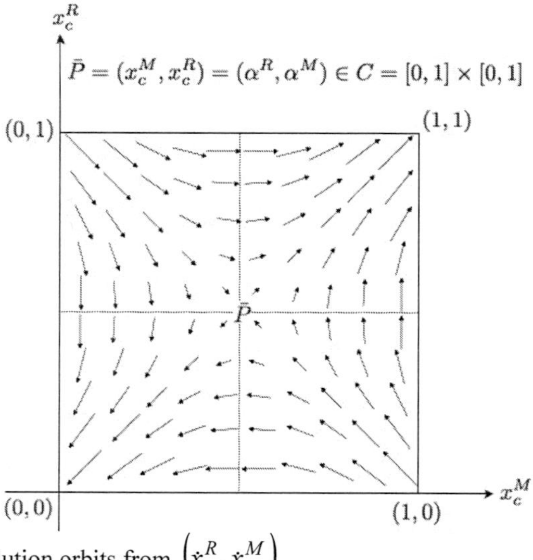

Figure 3-1. Solution orbits from $\left(\dot{x}_c^R, \dot{x}_c^M\right)$

Note that, the hypothetical location of the point $\overline{P} = (\overline{x}_c^R, \overline{x}_c^M)$ looks at the center of the $\mathbf{C}$ − square, but this is not necessarily its real location, since it depends on the values α^R and α^M which are the constant terms of the reviewing decision $r_i^\tau(x) = f_i^\tau(u_i^\tau)$ of switching behavior.

3.6. Concluding Remarks

We have shown that imitative behavior can be represented by the replicator dynamics with two specific cases: (i) pure imitation driven by dissatisfaction, where all reviewing agents imitate the first person they encounter, and (ii) the successful reviewing strategist chooses the actions with the best payoffs, with a probability proportional to the expected payoff.

As long as the linear approximation is mathematically valid, the second differs from the first, yet we obtain similar evolutionary dynamics for the two models. Similar conclusions can be applied to the relationship between ESS, Nash equilibrium and the Replicator Dynamics.

Hence, we conclude that for imitation rules which use random sampling, **whom an agent imitates is more important than how an agent imitates**. We justify the extension of the simpler model based on a description of an observed behavior: agents choose an expected maximization of benefits, since *they do what others do when they can imitate successful strategies*.

We have introduced the concept of ESS for a model of two asymmetric populations and we have shown that for every ESS, there is a strict Nash equilibrium and the converse. For further characterization results on the set of Evolutionarily Stable Strategies and Nash equilibrium, we refer the reader to Balkenborg and Schlag (2007) and the texts by Van Damme (1991) or Vega-Redondo (1996) and Weibull (1995).

Finally, we have presented a specific form of the behavioral rule, in which agents imitate according to the best performed strategy when they meet agents performing better than they do. We have shown that imitation is represented by the replicator dynamic system, since agents do what others do by imitating successful strategies. We have characterized the evolutionarily stable strategies of the replicator dynamics. Thus we must add a caveat to our original conclusion: who an agent imitates is more important than how an agent imitates, but the specific ‘how’ that an agent adopts can affect their relative success too.

CHAPTER FOUR

THE EVOLUTION OF POVERTY TRAPS

This chapter proposes a coordination game between two different types of economic agents: the high and low profile economic agents. The agents follow an imitative behavior supporting two asymetric populations and thus they adopt actions conforming to a convention (see Sanchez Carrera, 2012; Accinelli and Sanchez Carrera, 2012).

Samuel Bowles (2006) pointed out the notion of institutional poverty traps, meaning that an institution is composed as one of a number of possible conventions. From equilibria in which members of a population typically act in ways that maximize payoffs, given the actions taken by others and in which agents' hold beliefs about what others will do, these factors support continued adherence to conventional actions. A convention is thus an outcome in which it is in the interest of agents to adhere to the convention as long as they believe that most others will do the same. Because a convention is one of many possible mutually best responses, institutions are not environmentally determined, but rather are of human construction (but not necessarily of deliberate design). Conventions are self-enforcing; that is, they are evolutionarily stable as a result of the positive feedback associated with members conforming to a common strategy. Consequently, institutions that take the form of conventions will display inertia, and transitions among them will occur rapidly but infrequently, displaying a pattern that biologists call punctuated equilibria (see Eldredge and Gould, 1972). Hence, the next model is on the notion of institutional poverty traps from a coordination game in an evolutionary game theoretical framework.

4.1. The Game

Let us allow economic agents to be either leaders, (1), or followers, (2), with two different types: high- or low-profile. The vectors $(H,L);(h,l)$ are the strategy spaces, S_i, denoting high- and low-profiles types of leaders and followers, $i = 1, 2$.[17]

Let us assume that a contractual period is characterized by:

1) **Strategic complementarities**. In this economy, in order to profit, player 1 must employ player 2 under strategic complementarity, in the sense that the $H-$type agent matching with an $h-$type is more profitable than matching with an $l-$ type. Analogously, the $L-$type agent matching with an $l-$type is more profitable than matching with an $h-$type.
   i) A gross income of 1 being an $H-$type is U or u, and of being an $L-$type is V or v, which depends on matching with high- or low-profile followers.
   ii) A gross income of 2 is W when hired by H and w when is hired by L.
   iii) Agents 1 and 2 face income taxes γ and τ .
2) **Private information**. The leader knows the types of the followers, but the followers do not know the type of the leaders and they assume with probability σ that they will be hired by a leader of $H-$type and with probability $(1-\sigma)$ by an $L-$type.
   a) Choosing between high- and low-profiles does not have any cost for the leader; while if the follower decides to become an $h-$type, they incur a training cost or the cost of education C, and if they decide to be an $l-$type, this does not incur any costs.
3) At the end of the contractual period, the $H-$type leader must give a signal p to the $h-$type follower.[18] Such a signal can be viewed as giving some skill premium, bonus, or efficiency wage, which are perceived only by $h-$type followers and received at the end of the contractual period.

The *strategic form representation* is:

$$\Gamma = \{i, S = \{(H, L); (h, l)\}, E^i_{s_i}(\cdot)\}$$

where $E^i_{s_i}(\cdot)$ is the expected payoff of player *i*. The payoff matrix is:

[17] Leader and follower games are described by imperfect information in which the leader moves first, knowing the type of the follower, but then followers are the second movers without knowing the type of the leader (see Fudenberg and Tirole, 1991).

[18] Signaling games are incomplete information leader-follower games in which only the leader has private information (see Fudenberg and Tirole, 1991).

$2 \backslash 1$	H	L
h	$(1-\tau)W+p-C,\ (1-\gamma)U-W-p$	$(1-\tau)w-C,\ (1-\gamma)v-w$
l	$(1-\tau)W,\ (1-\gamma)u-W$	$(1-\tau)w,\ (1-\gamma)V-w$

Note that, the premium or bonus P, is bounded on,

- $p > C > 0$, incentives to be a high-profile follower and it is payoff dominant for a low-profile follower, or,
$$0 < C-(1-\tau)(w-W) < p.$$
This means that $h-$type followers must get a bonus greater than the net difference of wages to being high- or low-profile.
- The $H-$ type leaders cannot give a bonus or efficiency wage greater than the net difference of gains to being high- or low-profile:
$$p < (1-\gamma)(U-u).$$
- By complementarities, the $H-$ type prefers a $h-$type follower because:
$$(1-\gamma)(U-v) > W-w+p,$$

and the $L-$type prefers an $l-$type:
$$(1-\gamma)(V-u) > w-W.$$

Hence, the game has two pure Nash equilibria:
$$(H,h)=(1,0;1,0) \text{ and } (L,l)=(0,1;0,1),$$
where the strategy pair (H,h) payoff dominates (L,l) while (L,l) risk dominates (H,h). There is a mixed strategy Bayesian Nash equilibrium given by,
$$(\theta,(1-\theta);\ \sigma,(1-\sigma)),$$
where θ is the leader's probability of matching a high-type follower, and σ is the follower's probability of matching a high-type leader. That is,
$$\sigma = \frac{C}{p} \text{ and } \theta = \frac{(1-\gamma)(V-u)+W-w}{(1-\gamma)(U-u+V-v)-p}.$$
This is because our model can be studied as an extensive-form game, with a finite game tree consisting of nodes X. Let $z \in Z \subset X$ be the terminal nodes. A pure strategy for player $i \in (1,2)$, s_i, is an action at each node in $x \in X_i$, $s_i(x) \in S = \{(H,L);(h,l)\}$.

We can now find the self-confirming equilibria (SCE), since they are based on the idea that players should have correct beliefs about probability distributions that they observe sufficiently often (Fudenberg and Levine, 2007). We suppose that all players know the structure of the extensive form, so that each player knows the space S of strategy profiles. Each player i receives a payoff in the stage game that depends on the terminal node. Player i's payoff function is denoted $\pi_i \ : \ Z \rightarrow \mathrm{R}$. Let $\Delta(\cdot)$ denote the space of probability distributions over a set. Then a mixed strategy profile is $\Phi \in \Delta(S_1) \times \Delta(S_2)$. Let the nodes that are reached with positive probability under Φ be denoted by $\overline{X}(\Phi)$.

A Nash equilibrium requires that players have correct beliefs about the strategies their opponents use to map their types to their actions. In order for repeated observations to lead players to learn the distribution of opponents' strategies, the signals observed at the end of each round of play must be sufficiently informative. Each player has a belief about his opponents' play. Let μ_i denote the belief of player i on the probability distribution over feasible actions, $\sigma_i(x) \in \Delta(\cdot)$. Player i's belief is correct at an opponent j's node x if $\mu_i(\{\sigma_{-i} \mid \sigma_j(x) = \sigma^{\phi}(x)\}) = 1$.

Hence, SCE assumes that the players' inferences are consistent with their observations, which are consistent with the Perfect Bayesian Equilibria (PBE).[19]

> Definition 12. ***(Fudenberg & Levine, 2007.)*** *The mixed strategy profile Φ is a heterogenous self-confirming equilibrium if, for each player, $i = 1, 2$ and for each strategy s_i with $\hat{\sigma}_i(s_i) > 0$ there are beliefs μ_i such that*
>
> - *s_i is a best response to $\mu_i(s_i)$ and*
> - *$\mu_i(s_i)$ is correct at every node reached with positive probability under $\hat{\Phi}_{-i}$, $x \in \overline{X}(s_i, \Phi)$.*

Given that all information sets are always reached, self-confirming equilibria are equivalent to Nash equilibria. Thus σ cannot be chosen

[19]Recall that PBE involves optimal actions given beliefs and consistent beliefs in equilibrium (Fudenberg and Tirole, 1991). In cases where more than one PBE is possible, it is also appropriate to examine whether some can be ruled out. In some cases, PBEs rely on unreasonable beliefs that are technically sustainable (because they are off the equilibrium path of behavior) but unlikely to persist if people deviate slightly from equilibrium predictions.

exogenously, but must be determined in equilibrium. Formally, equilibrium $\{H,h\}$ is self-confirming for any value that is a large enough value of σ, since, it is supported by player 1 believing that player 2 will play h and player 2 believing that player 1 will play *H*. That is, assume that player 1 picks an action *H* and 2 believes in it with $\mu_2(\sigma)=\sigma$. Then, her expected payoff, E_h^2, is given by,

$$E_h^2 = \sigma\big((1-\tau)W + p\big) + (1-\sigma)(1-\tau)w - C.$$

Alternatively, when 2 is choosing $l-$type,

$$E_l^2 = (1-\tau)\big(\sigma W + (1-\sigma)w\big).$$

Thus, 2 prefers to be an $h-$type strategist if $E_h^2 > E_l^2$, and it happens if and only if σ is large enough, i.e.

$$\sigma \geq \frac{C}{p},$$

where $\frac{C}{p} \in (0,1)$ is interpreted as a ratio of "education costs–skill premium". Player 2's best response to $H-$type is h and $\sigma=1$, which is consistent with the fact that $\sigma > \frac{C}{p}$, hence it is an SCE. Analogously, Player 2's best response to $L-$type 1 is l if $\sigma < \frac{C}{p}$ and $\sigma = 0$, which is consistent with $\sigma < \frac{C}{p}$, and then it is an SCE. Therefore, equilibria $\left\{H,h,\sigma \geq \frac{C}{p}\right\}$ and $\left\{L,l,\sigma < \frac{C}{p}\right\}$ are heterogeneous SCE.

The next section analyzes this game as an evolutionary process. Recall that the term *evolutionary process* means that more successful types tend to proliferate while less successful types tend to disappear, an assumption that applies equally well to learning by imitation and cultural evolution as well as to literal population replacement by natural selection.

4.2. The Evolutionary Game

The simplest setting in which to study learning is one in which agents' strategies are completely observed at the end of each round, and agents are randomly matched with a series of anonymous opponents so that the agents have no impact on what they observe. Hereafter, populations of leaders (1) and followers (2) are denoted by X^1 and X^2, and the populations are composed of a large number of agents that face the problem of selecting a profile based on the corresponding: $\{H,L\}$; $\{h,l\}$. Let us denote a fraction of agents of each sub-population as

$$x_i^k = \frac{X_i^k}{X^k}, \tag{4.1}$$

for all pairs $i \in \{(H,L);(h,l)\}$ of sub-population $k \in \{1,2\}$. That is, the share of $h-$type strategists is

$$x_h^2 = \frac{X_h^2}{X_h^2 + X_l^2} \tag{4.2}$$

where $X_h^2 + X_l^2 = X^2$ is assumed to be a constant. Assume that both populations are normalized to 1, $x_H^1 + x_L^1 = 1$ and $x_h^2 + x_l^2 = 1$. Hence, the probabilities $\sigma = x_H^1$ and $\theta = x_h^2$, and thus, the expected payoffs can be written as

$$E_h^2 = x_H^1\left((1-\tau)W + p\right) + (1 - x_H^1)(1-\tau)w - C \tag{4.3}$$

$$E_l^2 = x_H^1(1-\tau)W + (1 - x_H^1)(1-\tau)w \tag{4.4}$$

$$E_H^1 = x_h^2\left((1-\gamma)U - W - p\right) + (1 - x_h^2)\left((1-\gamma)u - W\right) \tag{4.5}$$

$$E_L^1 = x_h^2\left((1-\gamma)v - w\right) + (1 - x_h^2)\left((1-\gamma)V - w\right) \tag{4.6}$$

Let us consider the *n*-population replicator dynamics (Weibull, 1995:172) suggested by Taylor (1979) of the form,

$$\dot{x}_i^k = \left[E_i^k - \bar{E}^k\right]x_i^k, \tag{4.7}$$

where $x_i^k \in [0,1]$ and $\dot{x}_i^k + \dot{x}_j^k = 0$ for all pairs $i \neq j \in \{(H,L)(h,l)\}$ of population $k \in \{1,2\}$.[20] In other words, the growth rate $\dot{x}_i^k / x_i^k$ of the associated population share is equal its excess payoff, $E_i^k - \overline{E}^k$, over the average payoff in its player population:

$$\overline{E}^k = \frac{X_i^k}{X^k} \cdot E_i^k + \frac{X_j^k}{X^k} \cdot E_j^k. \tag{4.8}$$

In the following, we argue that if followers and leaders decide to imitate successful strategists, and if the state of the economy is such that playing high-profile is the successful strategy, then the economy converges to the high-level equilibrium. Otherwise, if the state of the economy is one in which being low-profile is the successful strategy, then the economy will be caught in a poverty trap.

4.2.1 Replication by Imitation

Consider an *i*-type agent, $i \in \{(H,L);(h,l)\}$, from population $k \in \{1,2\}$, who reviews her strategy with probability $r_i^k(x)$ to consider whether she should or should not change her current strategy, where

$$x = \left(\left(x_H^1, x_L^1\right), \left(x_h^2, x_l^2\right)\right)$$

is the current profiles' distribution.

Assume that an agent's decision depends upon the expected payoff associated with her own behavior, s_i,[21] given the composition of the opposite population, labeled as $E_i^k(s_i, x^{-k})$, $\forall i \in \{h,l;H,L\}$, of sub-population $k,-k \in \{1,2\}, k \neq -k$.

Hence, $r_i^k(x)$ is the average time-rate at which an agent that currently uses strategy *i* reviews her strategy choice. Then,

$$r_i^k(x) = f_i^k\left(E_i^k(s_i, x^{-k}), x\right) \in [0,1]. \tag{4.9}$$

---

[20]It assures that the trajectory $x^k(t) = \left\{(x_i^k(t), x_j^k(t)),\ t_0 \leq t\right\}$ is bounded in the unit square $C = [0,1] \times [0,1]$.

[21] $s_i = \{(H,L);(h,l)\}$ indicates vectors of pure strategies independently from population *k*.

As before, the function $f_i^k(\cdot)$ is interpreted as the propensity of a member from the *i*-th club to consider switching membership as a function of the expected utility gains from such a choice. Agents with less successful strategies on average review their strategy at a higher rate than agents with more successful strategies.

Having opted for a change, the agent will adopt the strategy followed by the first person of her population to be encountered (her neighbor), i. e., for any $k \in \{1,2\}$, $p_{ij}^k(x)$ is the probability that a reviewing *i*-strategist changes to some pure strategy $j \neq i$, $\forall \ j \in \{(H,L);(h,l)\}$.

The *outflow* from club i in population k is $x_i^k r_i^k(x) p_{ij}^k(x)$ and the *inflow* is $x_j^k r_j^k(x) p_{ji}^k(x)$. Then, $\forall \ j \neq i \in \{(H,L);(h,l)\}$, $k \in \{1,2\}$; by the law of large numbers we model these processes as deterministic flows and, rearranging terms, we obtain

$$x_i^k = x_k^j \left[f_j^k \left(E_j^k(s_j, x^{-k}) \right) p_{ji}^k(x) \right] - x_i^k \left[f_i^k \left(E_i^k(s_i, x^{-k}) \right) p_{ij}^k(x) \right] \qquad (4.10)$$

System (4.10) represents the interaction between two groups of agents that imitate their neighbors. By the normalization rule, $x_H^1 + x_L^1 = 1$ and $x_h^2 + x_l^2 = 1$, system (4.10) can be reduced to two equations with two independent state variables.

Once again, assume $f_i^k(\cdot)$ to be population specific and to be linear in utility levels (see Weibull, 1995). Thus, the propensity to switch behavior is decreasing in the level of the expected utility; that is, $\forall \ j \neq i \in \{(H,L);(h,l)\}$, $k \in \{1,2\}$, we get

$$f_i^k \left(E_i^k(s_i, x^{-k}) \right) = \alpha^k - \boldsymbol{\beta}^k E_i^k(s_i, x^{-k}), \qquad (4.11)$$

where α^k, $\boldsymbol{\beta}^k \geq 0$ and $\frac{\alpha^k}{\boldsymbol{\beta}^k} \geq^k E_i^k(s_i, x^{-k})$ assures that $f_i^k(\cdot) \in [0,1]$. The parameter α^k can be interpreted as a degree of dissatisfaction and $\boldsymbol{\beta}^k$ measures the performance of their own payoff on reviewing the current strategy. As far as the payoff level of the $i-$strategist, as $E_i^k(\cdot)$ increases, her average reviewing rate, $r_i^k(x)$, will decrease.

Recall the average rule where each strategy is evaluated according to the average payoff observed in the reference group (see J. Apesteguia et al., 2007). Consider that economic agents do not know the exact payoffs of their corresponding neighbors, but they can compute some average payoffs in their neighborhoods and they can imitate the behavior that yields the highest average payoff.

Although an agent does not know all the true values of the payoff of the others, she can take a sample of such true values in order to estimate the average. Let $\widetilde{E}_i^k$ and $\widetilde{E}_j^k$ be the estimators for the true values E_i^k and E_j^k. Hence, the process of copying successful behaviors exhibits *payoff monotonic updating*, since strategies with above-average payoffs are adopted by others and thus increase their share in the population; that is, each $i-$strategist changes her strategy if and only if $\widetilde{E}_i^k < \widetilde{E}_j^k$.

Let us apply the behavioral rule given in Definition 11 from Chapter 3 where a reviewing strategist, *i*, who decides to change her current strategy must take into consideration: (i) the probability of imitating one strategy which performs better than her current strategy, $P[\widetilde{E}_i^k(s_j, x^{-k}) < \widetilde{E}_j^k(s_i, x^{-k})]$, and (ii) the probability of meeting an agent, x_j^k, who currently uses such a strategy. Therefore, for any pair $i \neq j \in \{(H,L);(h,l)\}$, $k \in \{1,2\}$,

$$p_{ij}^k(x) = \begin{cases} \lambda E_j^k(\cdot) x_j^\tau & \text{if } E_j^k(\cdot) > 0 \\ 0 & \text{if } E_j^k(\cdot) \leq 0 \end{cases}$$

and

$$p_{ji}^k(x) = \begin{cases} \lambda E_i^k(\cdot) x_i^\tau & \text{if } E_i^k(\cdot) > 0 \\ 0 & \text{if } E_i^k(\cdot) \leq 0 \end{cases}$$

where $\lambda = \frac{1}{E_i^k(\cdot) + E_j^k(\cdot)}$.

Hence, by the above considerations, system (4.10) becomes the system of replicator dynamic equations driven by imitation, i.e.,

$$\dot{x}_i^k = x_i^k(1 - x_i^k)\lambda\left[\left(\alpha^k - \boldsymbol{\beta}^k E_j^k(\cdot)\right) - \left(\alpha^k - \boldsymbol{\beta}^k E_i^k(\cdot)\right)\right] \tag{4.12}$$

by substitution of the expected payoffs (equations 4.3-4.6), and after some algebraic manipulation, we get:

$$\begin{cases} \dot{x}_h^2 = -\dot{x}_l^2 = x_h^2\left(1 - x_h^2\right)[A(\cdot)] \\ \\ \dot{x}_H^1 = -\dot{x}_1^L = x_H^1(1 - x_H^1)[B(\cdot)] \end{cases}$$

where the functions $A(\cdot)$ and $B(\cdot)$ are defined as:

$$A(\cdot) = \frac{\beta^2\left(px_H^1 - C\right)}{2\left(x_H^1 W + (1 - x_H^1)w\right)(1 - \tau) + px_H^1 - C},$$

$$B(\cdot) = \frac{\beta^1\left(x_h^2((v - U)(1 - \gamma) - p) - \left(1 - x_h^2\right)(1 - \gamma)u - V\left(\left(1 - x_h^2\right) - \left(1 - x_h^2\right)\gamma\right) - W + w\right)}{x_h^2((1 - \gamma)(U + v) - W - w - p) + (1 - x_h^2)((1 - \gamma)(V + u) - W - w)}.$$

The system $\left(\dot{x}_h^2, \dot{x}_H^1\right)$ describes the case where strategies propagate via imitation, and expected payoffs drive the rate of imitation, reinforcement, and inhibition of the behaviors of the high-profile agents from the populations of leaders 1 and followers 2.

The system $\left(\dot{x}_h^2, \dot{x}_H^1\right)$ admits five stationary states or dynamic equilibria, i.e. (0,0), (0,1), (1,0), (1,1) and a positive interior equilibrium $\left(x_H^{1^*}, x_h^{2^*}\right)$,

where the interesting case is the equilibrium $\overline{P} = \left(x_H^{1^*}, x_h^{2^*}\right)$ given by:

$$x_H^{1^*} = \frac{C}{p},$$

$$x_h^{2^*} = \frac{(1 - \gamma)(V - u) + W - w}{(1 - \gamma)(U - u + V - v) - p}.$$

The trivial equilibrium is one where leaders and followers are all low-profile economic agents; that is, the pure strategic profile: $(L, l) = (0,1;0,1) = (0,0)$. On the other hand, in the opposite corner, there is the case where all agents are high-profile; that is, the pure strategic profile: $(H, h) = (1,0;1,0) = (1,1)$. The two remaining border equilibria, which are not Nash equilibria, show a different club dominating the two populations, and in a sense, a mismatch between strategies $\{L, h\}$, $\{H, l\}$ or $(0,1)$, $(1,0)$. The interior equilibrium is composed of marriages among low- or high-profile economic agents: $\overline{P} = \left(x_H^{1^*}, x_h^{2^*}\right)$.

4.3. ESSs and Evolutionary Dynamics

To observe the dynamics of the game, we calculate trajectories, i.e. how the mixed strategies change. We start with any pair of mixed strategies $\left(x_2^h, x_1^H\right)$ and calculate the dynamics given by the system $\left(\dot{x}_h^2, \dot{x}_H^1\right)$ as we progress along a certain trajectory. Let us recall the following definitions:

> Definition 13. *A "trajectory" is a path determined in the phase space of the solution of a dynamical system passing through a given point of the space at a given time.*

> Definition 14. *An "attractor" of a dynamical system is a subset of the state space to which orbits originating from typical initial conditions tend as time increases.*

> Definition 15. *A "saddle point" is a fixed point that has at least one positive eigenvalue and one negative eigenvalue in its linearization; more generally, a fixed point for which there are trajectories that tend to the fixed point in both positive and negative time. That is, a saddle point is a point whose stable and unstable manifolds have a dimension which is not zero.*

> Definition 16. *The "basin of attraction" of an attractor is the set of initial conditions as a region in the state space leading to long-time behavior that approaches to the attractor.*

Thus the qualitative behavior of the long-time motion of a given system can be fundamentally different depending on which basin of attraction the initial condition lies in (e.g., attractors can correspond to periodic, quasiperiodic or chaotic behaviors of different types). Regarding a basin of attraction as a region in the state space, it has been found that the basic topological structure of such regions can vary greatly from system to system.

Another important concept is that of evolutionarily stable strategy (ESS). A population playing such a strategy is uninvadable by any other strategy. Uninvadability is a useful characterization of evolutionary stability, and indeed its original definition is that a strategy x^* is evolutionarily stable if and only if (a) it is a best response to itself, and (b) it is a better response to all other best responses than they are to themselves. By definition, no alternative best response exists for any player population if the profile in question x^* happens to be a strict Nash equilibrium, so such profiles should qualify. In other words, consider a two-population normal form game:

$$\Gamma = \left\{\tau \in \{1,2\}, \left((H,L);(h,l)\right), E^\tau(\cdot)\right\}$$

where each population has two possible behaviors, (H,L) and (h,l), denoting high- and low-profiles types of leaders (1) and followers (2) with expected payoffs $E^{\tau}(\cdot)$. Then:

Definition 17. *A strategy* $x \in \Delta^{\tau}$ *is an ESS in asymmetric games like* Γ, *for a population* τ *if and only if*

$$E^{\tau}(x_i, y_{-i}) \geq E^{\tau}(z_i, y_{-i}) \ \forall\, z \in \Delta^{\tau}$$

and for all $y' \in \Delta,\ y' \neq y$ *there exists some* $\bar{\varepsilon}_{y'} \in (0,1)$, *such that for all* $\varepsilon \in (0, \bar{\varepsilon}_{y'})$ *and with* $w_{\varepsilon} = \varepsilon y' + (1-\varepsilon) y$,

$$E^{\tau}(x_i, w_{\varepsilon}) > E^{\tau}(y_i, w_{\varepsilon}), \quad \forall\, \tau \in \{1,2\}.$$

Intuitively, we say that *x* is an ESS if and only if after a mutation in population $-\tau$ continues to be a best response for the post-entry population, w_{ε}.

Zeeman (1992) shows that an ESS is asymptotically stable (AS) in the replicator dynamics, such that trajectories do not necessarily have to settle at the equilibrium (which would be neutrally stable) to be an ESS (more details in Weibull, 1995), but the converse of this statement is not necessarily true, and AS does not imply ESS. Then, for asymmetric games with strategic complementarities, the notion of ESS against the field is more useful. An evolutionarily stable strategy (ESS) against the field is a mixed-Nash equilibrium that is uninvadable by any alternative strategy into the basin of attraction. That is:

Definition 18. *Consider that the profile distribution from population* 1 *is given by* $x^1 = \left(x_H^1, x_L^1\right)$, *then we say that the strategy* $\bar{x}^2 = \left(\bar{x}_H^2, \bar{x}_L^2\right)$ *is an* ***ESS against the field*** *of* x^1 *if there exists* $\varepsilon_{x^1} > 0$ *such that:*

$$E^2\left(\bar{x}^2, \bar{x}^1\right) \geq E^2\left(x^2, \bar{x}^1\right)$$

for all $x^2 \in S_2$ *where* $\left|x^1 - \bar{x}^1\right| \leq \varepsilon_{x^1}$.

Nevertheless, by complementarities, it can happen that the field – defined by the strategy or the profile distribution from one population, which the opponent takes as given – evolves at the same time under the pressures in the changes of distribution generated by such opponents. Then, such interdependence of behaviors can generate ESS in both populations. For that reason, we should consider the definition of *ESS against the field for strategic profiles*:

Definition 19. ***(Evolutionarily stable strategic profile)*** *A strategic profile* $(x^1,...,x^n)$ *is evolutionarily stable, if* x^i *defines for all* $i=1,...,n$ *an ESS against the field* x^{-i} *being* $x^{-i}=(x^1,...,x^{i-1},x^{i+1},...,x^n)$ *generated by the strategic behavior of all the other opponents.*

Hence, if an economic system evolves into a poverty trap, then any small perturbation in the initial conditions are not enough to lead the system outside the basin of attraction from the distribution that defines the poverty trap. This means that the poverty trap is an attractor of trajectories defined by probability distributions that are evolutionarily stable strategic profiles. The following proposition summarizes our main results:

Proposition. *By imitation of agents, the evolutionary dynamics from the system* $\left(\dot{x}_h^2,\dot{x}_H^1\right)$, *is as follows:*

i) Equilibria $(0,0)$ *and* $(1,1)$ *are asymptotically stable points and define the strategic profiles* $(0,1;0,1)$ *and* $(1,0;1,0)$ *respectively, and they are ESS against the field into their basin of attraction.*

ii) Equilibrium $\overline{P}=\left(x_H^{1^*},x_h^{2^*}\right)$ *is a threshold, since, it separates the basins of attraction of the low-level and high-level equilibria and, with the exception of a single curve through this point, all solution trajectories converge to the attractors.*

Proof. Consider the Jacobean associated to the system $\left(\dot{x}_h^2,\dot{x}_H^1\right)$, given by,

$$J(\cdot)=\begin{pmatrix}(1-2x_h^2)\left(x_H^1p-C\right) & x_h^2(1-x_h^2)p\\ x_H^1(1-x_H^1)(1-\gamma)(U-u+V-v) & \left(1-2x_H^1\right)K\end{pmatrix}, \tag{4.13}$$

where $K=x_h^2((1-\gamma)(\Delta U+\Delta V))-(1-\gamma)(V+u)-W+w$. Equilibria fitting $\det(J)>0$ and $tr(J)<0$ (i.e. eigenvalues having negative real parts) are uniformly hyperbolic attractors because the trajectories that converge to them are not elliptical trajectories, and from Definition 18, they are ESSs against the field. Therefore, we should evaluate $J\left(\dot{x}_h^2,\dot{x}_H^1\right)$:

1) $x_h^2=x_H^1=0$. The evaluated Jacobean in this case is given by,

$$J = \begin{bmatrix} -C & 0 \\ 0 & -\left((1-\gamma)(V+u)+W-w\right) \end{bmatrix}.$$

It yields $\det J = (W - w + (1-\gamma)(V+u))(C) > 0$ and $trJ < 0$. Hence this equilibrium point $(0,0)$ is an attractor and therefore an ESS.

2) $x_h^2 = x_H^1 = 1$. The evaluated Jacobean is given by,

$$J = \begin{bmatrix} -(p-C) & 0 \\ 0 & -\left(W - w + (1-\gamma)(U - 2u - v)\right) \end{bmatrix}.$$

Thus, $\det J > 0$ and $trJ < 0$. Hence this equilibrium point $(1,1)$ is an attractor and an ESS.

3) $x_h^2 = 1$, $x_H^1 = 0$. The evaluated Jacobean is,

$$J = \begin{bmatrix} C & 0 \\ 0 & (1-\gamma)(U-2u-v)-W+w \end{bmatrix}.$$

Thus, $\det J > 0$ and $trJ > 0$. In this case, the equilibrium point $(1,0)$ is a repulsor.

4) $x_h^2 = 0$, $x_H^1 = 1$. The evaluated Jacobean in this case is,

$$J = \begin{bmatrix} p-C & 0 \\ 0 & (1-\gamma)(V+u)+W-w \end{bmatrix}.$$

Thus, $\det J > 0$ and $trJ > 0$. In this case, the equilibrium point $(0,1)$ is a repulsor.

Since, the $\mathbf{C}$ – square is partitioned into four regions, the point $\left(x_h^{2^*}, x_H^{1^*}\right)$ is a saddle and the other four are local attractors or repulsors. The curve that converges to $\overline{P}$ is a set of critical values into the state of the $\mathbf{C}$ – square with the following property: the optimal strategy is different depending on which side of the threshold the current state lies. Therefore, there is just a one-dimensional manifold (threshold level) which goes through $\overline{P}$. Such a threshold separates the basins of attraction into $(0,0)$ and $(1,1)$. Hence, if the initial distribution of high-profile economic agents is lower that the threshold $\left(x_h^{2^*}, x_H^{1^*}\right)$, then the strategic profile $(L,l) = (0,1;0,1)$ is an ESS against the field of $\left(\overline{x}_h^2, \overline{x}_H^1\right)$ for all $\left(\overline{x}_h^2, \overline{x}_H^1\right) \neq \left(x_h^{2^*}, x_H^{1^*}\right) \in \Delta^k$. Otherwise, when the threshold has been overcome, the equilibrium $(H,h) = (1,0;1,0)$ is an ESS against the field.

In other words:

a) Consider a pair of initial distributions $x_0 = (x_0^1, x_0^2) \in \Delta^1 \times \Delta^2$ such that the corresponding values of the high-profiles are lower than $\bar{P} = \left(x_H^{1^*}, x_h^{2^*}\right)$; then, the economy will evolve on trajectories defined by the solutions of the system $\left(\dot{x}_h^2, \dot{x}_H^1\right)$, where $(0,1) \in \Delta^1$ is a best response for $x^2(t)$ and $(0,1) \in \Delta^2$ is a best response for $x^1(t)$, and $(x^1(t), x2(t))$ is the solution for the system $\left(\dot{x}_h^2, \dot{x}_H^1\right)$ with the initial conditions (x_0^1, x_0^2). Moreover, it holds that $x^1(t) \rightarrow (0,1)$ and $x^2(t) \rightarrow (0,1)$ with $t \rightarrow \infty$. Then, the whole economy converges to the attractor $(0,1;0,1)$.

b) But if the initial conditions of the economy defined by $(x_0^1, x_0^2) \in \Delta^1 \times \Delta^2$ are such that the initial values of profile distributions x_{H0}^1 and x_{h0}^2 are larger than $\bar{P}$, then we obtain trajectories such that the economy converges to $(1,0,1,0)$.

Figure 4-1 draws the evolutionary dynamics for the replicator dynamics by imitation $\left(x_h^{2^*}, x_H^{1^*}\right)$.

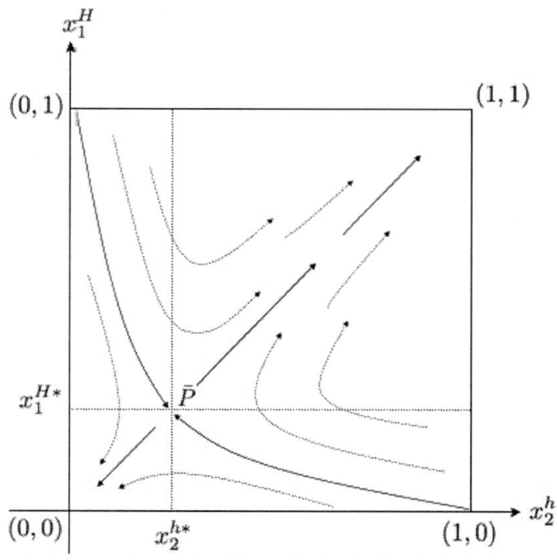

Figure 4-1. Evolutionary dynamics driven by imitative behavior.

Note that the location of the saddle point $\overline{P}$ depends on the parameters' values: education costs, premia or bonuses and income taxes.

4.4 To Overcome the Poverty Trap

The following statement emphasizes our notion of the poverty trap: Equilibrium $(0,0)$ is a poverty trap in the sense that an economy starting with a (sufficiently) low number of high-profile agents experiences a decreasing sequence of high-profile economic agents that eventually leads to no high-profile agents. This is due to the rationality of the economic agents who are facing a population state (or an economy) where low-profile agents are the dominant strategies. Then, for such an economy, an imitative agent would decide to become a low-profile economic agent.

In terms of game theory:

Definition 20. *A **poverty trap** is a Nash equilibrium Pareto dominated, which is a steady state of the replicator dynamic system defined by the rules of conduct which define a local attractor, to which trajectories converge shaped by evolutionarily stable strategic profiles.*

For a large initial number of high-profile agents, greater than the level $\overline{P} = \left(x_1^{H^*}, x_2^{h^*}\right)$, the economy converges over time toward the sample path $t \to (1,1)$ of high-profile agents. To reduce the basin of attraction of the low-level equilibrium $(0,0)$, either $x_1^{H^*}$ or $x_2^{h^*}$ should decrease, i.e.,

1. The ratio of education costs–skill premia, $\frac{C}{p}$, decreases if the training costs C fall or the value of the premia p rises.
2. With fixed training costs, C, if the followers' probability of matching with a high-type leader, σ, decreases, then the number of high-profile followers is decreasing too. To avoid this situation, the value of p must be larger than C. For instance, if $\sigma = \frac{1}{2} \geq \frac{C}{p}$, the bonus should be twice as large as the training costs, $p \geq 2C$. Hence, when the number of high-profile followers is small, the skill premia p should be large enough in order to incentivise the other agents to switch their current behavior and to join the club of high-profile followers.
   a) Decreasing the value of $x_1^{H^*}$: either training costs C should decrease, or the bonus p must increase, i.e.,

either, $\lim_{C \to 0} x_1^{H^*}$ or $\lim_{p \to \infty} x_1^{H^*} \Rightarrow x_1^{H^*} = 0.$

Hence, it fully expands the basin of attraction to $(1,1)$ which is the high-level equilibrium.

b) Moreover, income taxes γ play a crucial role in decreasing the value $x_2^{h^*}$:
   i. Assume that $\gamma \to 1$ (i.e., complete intervention of policy makers), then,
   $$\lim_{\gamma \to 1} x_2^{h^*} = -\frac{(W-w)}{p}.$$
   ii. Instead if $\gamma \to 0$ (non-intervention), then,
   $$\lim_{\gamma \to 0} x_2^{h^*} = \frac{u - V - (W - w)}{p - (V - v) - (U - u)}.$$
   iii. In fact, the value of γ which minimizes to zero $x_2^{h^*}$ is,
   $$\gamma = \frac{u - V - (W - w)}{u - V} \Rightarrow x_2^{h^*} = 0,$$
   which depends on the relations of followers' differential wages, $(W - w)$, and on the gross-utilities of the H – type leader, u , matching an l – type follower and the L – type leader, V , matching an l – type follower.

Hence, to overcome the poverty trap requires exogenous changes like reductions in training costs (or education costs) and increments of skill premia (or bonuses) and these can be implemented, for instance, by a fiscal policy on γ such that this encourages players to become high-profiles.

4.5 Concluding Remarks

We have studied an evolutionary game of the complementarity between the profiles of the economic agents. We show that the economy can be located in a low-level equilibrium and that an economy requires a threshold number of high-profile economic agents to overcome the poverty trap. Equilibrium $\{L, l\} = (0,1;0,1)$ or $(0,0)$, which is the low level equilibrium, is the most probable outcome in less developed countries during the early stages of development. It may often be interpreted as a poverty trap, as it is characterized by low levels of skills and a low technological profile. On the other hand, the high level equilibrium $\{H,h\}=(1,0;1,0)$ or (1,1) is generally found in developed countries in which the existence of low-profile economic agents may be negligible. The possibility of either high-level or low-level equilibria implies that agents acting under identical settings may experience either adequate living standards or deprivation (growth or crisis), and their result depends only on their history or initial conditions; that is, the composition of the state of the economy, depending on the initial number of high-profile agents.

The threshold level of the number of high-profile economic agents is a point $\overline{P}=\left(x_2^{h^*},x_1^{H^*}\right)$ separating paths leading to stable high and low level steady-states. Thus, this model can explain the coexistence of countries with low growth and countries with high growth as a function of their respective initial conditions alone.

Economies where the number of economic agents surpasses the threshold level $\overline{P}=\left(x_2^{h^*},x_1^{H^*}\right)$ can overcome the poverty trap, which is a latent possibility for any developing country. Such a threshold is mainly determined by training costs or education costs, bonuses or skill premia, and income taxes. Therefore, a policy maker may improve the state of the economy by means of these parameters.

CHAPTER FIVE

EVOLUTION AND COMPLEMENTARITIES OF FIRMS AND WORKERS

The aim of this chapter is to investigate the equilibrium/disequilibrium dynamics in an economy where two types of firms are present, innovative and non-innovative, and two types of workers are available in the labour market, high-skilled and low-skilled. Firstly, we consider that a worker's decision to be high or low-skilled is driven by imitative behavior; meanwhile, the initial distribution of innovative firms is taken as exogenous. But then, we consider that firms can also imitate in order to invest or not in innovation.

The model shows two possible equilibria: on one side there is the high-level equilibrium where a certain percentage of innovative firms is present in the economy, together with a definite percentage of high-skilled workers; on the other side, if the initial percentage of innovative firms is below a certain threshold, then the economy moves towards a low-level poverty trap equilibrium, where only non-innovative firms are present employing only low-skilled workers.

Hence, the main purpose of the present chapter is to explain the way in which an economy comprising different types of firms and workers can overcome low level equilibria, and to give some insights about which policies or main parameters a policy maker may consider in order to attain the high level equilibria and therefore sustained economic growth.

Even if our models are different to those studied by Nelson and Phelps (1966), or Redding (1996) and Acemoglu (1997; 1998), our results correspond to theirs. But, we find that the main factors to overcome the low level equilibria are when the agents act under imitative pressures, since they look at what their neighbors decide to do given the current state of the economy. Such factors are explained by lowering the cost of education and increasing the skill premia through tax incentives. Acemoglu (2009:9) summarized our insights clearly:

Economic growth will only take place if the society creates the institutions and policies that encourage innovation, reallocation, investment, and education. But such institutions should not be taken for granted.

Hence, it is the complementarity of human capital and innovation (R&D firms), and institutional attainment through agents' behavior that constitutes a way to overcome low level equilibria.

We state a model of two "players" considered innovative/non-innovative firms and skilled/unskilled workers, and they represent crucial issues nowadays in which policy-makers have to evaluate how much to invest. As stated, "the complementarity between R&D and human capital accumulation is widely accepted as an engine of sustained growth".

Then, two well known theories have to be considered. The first and more conventional one is "Skill-biased Technological Change" (see papers by Berman et al., 1994, in the US; Haskel and Heden, 1999, in the UK; and Machin and Van Reenen, 1998, extending to continental Europe) where investments in R&D, new products, new process and new technologies – even Information and Communication Technologies (ICTs) – increase the firms' demand for skilled workers, assuming that they have better knowledge of how to implement the new technologies (see the "absorptive capacity" by Cohen and Levinthal, 1990, p. 131 where "an organization's absorptive capacity will depend on the absorptive capacities of its individual members"). In this framework, skilled labour is a necessary complement to R&D activities in reinforcing the absorptive capacity of a given organization, and new technologies become more effective.

The second theory supports the endogeneity of the phenomenon, i.e. the endogenous skill-bias which suggests that skilled workers are responsible for inducing investments in new technologies in firms (see Kiley, 1999; Funk and Vogel, 2004).

Our approach is based on Accinelli and Sanchez Carrera (2011), firstly because we consider a model where workers' decisions are driven by imitative behavior and firms' decisions depend on the number of high-skilled workers. Secondly, we apply evolutionary game theory. Thus, let us start with the game.

5.1. The Game

Consider a two-player normal form game: a worker and a firm. The potential worker needs to decide whether to improve her skills or not. It can be hard to understand why and how a skilled worker can change her behavior to "non-skilled". Of course, this would depend on the kind of skills or knowledge under consideration and how the idea is motivated. Hence, we speak about the decision of being (or not) at the "frontier of knowledge". We assume that the workers' choice to be skilled or not can be decided by "imitation" – this means that every worker knows exactly the other workers' economic conditions and takes a training course with a 100% probability of being successful (but, of course, beginning a training course does not guarantee that the worker will pass it and find a skill-adequate job). Then, the firm needs to decide whether to invest in R&D or not, in order to become innovative firms or not. If a firm invests in R&D, it becomes innovative, if not, then it does not. Such decisions may depend on the current state of the economy. Thus if the economy is composed mainly of workers and firms with low-profiles, then potential workers and entrant firms decide not to invest in education and R&D departments.

Hence, we consider an economy composed of two populations: workers, W, and firms, F. Let us assume that each population is divided in two clubs:

- Every now and then, the $W-$population divided into the $S-$club that invests in improving their individual skills or in high-skilled workers, and the $NS-$club or low-skilled workers.
- Every now and then, the $F-$population divided into the $I-$club that invests in R&D or are innovative firms, and the $NI-$club of non-innovative firms.

The contractual period between types of firms and workers is described by:

- **Asymmetric information**. At the beginning of the contractual period, workers do not know the type of the firm that hired them. On the contrary, workers must certify their skill levels (for example, they must show a CV), and therefore firms know the type of the worker. Then, let us just consider that a worker will enter into a firm without understanding if the company invests in R&D or not; but it is more reasonable modeling that if an innovative firm is successful, the worker will get a premium.
- **Training costs and investment costs**. To become a high-skilled worker, an associated cost is involved. That is, the $S-$ type strategist must invest in education by, say, going to a training school, at an associated cost denoted CE. To become an innovative firm implies that the firm carries out investment in R&D departments at an associated cost denoted by CI.
- **Gross income**. Let $B_i(j)$ be the gross-benefit of the $i-$ firm

hiring the $j-$worker, $\forall \ i=\{I,NI\}, \ j=\{S,NS\}$. For all firms, the $S-$type worker gets a salary $\bar{s}$; instead, the $NS-$type worker gets a salary $s<\bar{s}$, $s\geq 0$.

- **Skill premia** [22] "Skill premia hypothesis" assumes that the innovative firms give premia to their workers (at the end of the contractual period). Assume that the innovative firms, I , give premia to their workers at the end of the contractual period, while $NI-$ firms do not share these benefits. [23] Thus, high-skilled workers, S , receive a premium $\bar{p}$ and low-skilled workers, NS , receive a premium p, $(0<p<\bar{p})$, when both are engaged with an innovative firm, I . Thus, $CE>\bar{s}$, i.e., if there are no prizes, there are no incentives to be a high-skilled worker. If $s\geq 0$ and $CE>\bar{s}$, $s\geq 0>\bar{s}-CE$.

Moreover, there are **strategic complementarities** between types of firms and workers.[24] Thus,

- If the firm is innovative, the payoff for the high-skilled worker is greater than the payoff for the low-skilled worker, i.e.: $\bar{s}+\bar{p}-CE>s+p$.
- If the firm is non-innovative, then the payoff for the low-skilled worker is at least as great as the payoff for the high-skilled worker, i.e.: $s\geq\bar{s}-CE$.
- If the worker is high-skilled, then the payoffs obtained by the innovative firm are greater than those obtained by the non-innovative firm, i.e., $B_I(S)-\bar{p}>B_{NI}(S)$.
- If the worker is low-skilled, then the benefits of the non-innovative firm are greater than those of the innovative firm, i.e.: $B_I(NS)-p<B_{NI}(NS)$.

---

[22]A seminal paper about the notion of skill premia is due by Acemoglu (2003).

[23]Recall that workers do not know the type of the contracting firm. So, at the beginning of the productive process, each worker does not know if she is going to receive a premium or not. This information is revealed only at the end of the period, once she learns the type of contracting firm.

[24]Two references on strategic complementarities among types of firms and workers are: 1) Acemoglu (1999): when there is a sufficient fraction of workers who are skilled, firms find it profitable to create jobs specifically targeted at this group, and as a result, unskilled wages fall and skilled wages increase. 2) Acemoglu (1998): as the economy accumulates more skills, technical change responds to make new technologies more complementary to skilled labor.

In summary, we have a two population normal form game. The payoff matrix for the game is represented by,

$W \mid F$	I	NI
S	$\bar{s}+\bar{p}-CE,\ B_I(S)-(\bar{s}+\bar{p}+CI)$	$\bar{s}-CE,\ B_{NI}(S)-\bar{s}$
NS	$s+p,\ B_I(NS)-(s+p+CI)$	$s,\ B_{NI}(NS)-s$

The expected payoffs of the $S-$type and $NS-$type strategist worker, given the probabilities of being hired either by the I or NI firms are denoted by $E(S)$ and $E(NS)$:

$$E(S)=\text{prob}(I)\left[\bar{s}+\bar{p}-CE\right]+\text{prob}(NI)(\bar{s})-CE \tag{5.1}$$

$$E(NS)=\text{prob}(I)\left[s+p\right]+\text{prob}(NI)s \tag{5.2}$$

where prob(I) represents the workers' probability of being hired by an innovative firm and prob(NI) represents being hired by a non-innovative firm. Hence, workers prefer to be an $S-$type strategist if $E(S)>E(NS)$, and the converse. This happens if and only if prob(I) is sufficiently large i.e.,

$$\text{prob}(I)>\frac{CE-(\bar{s}-s)}{(\bar{p}-p)}. \tag{5.3}$$

Workers are indifferent about being high-skilled or low-skilled if and only if,[25]

$$\text{prob}(I)=\frac{CE-(\bar{s}-s)}{(\bar{p}-p)}. \tag{5.4}$$

Let us denote the firms' probability of employing the high-skilled worker by prob(S) and let us use prob(NS) to denote employing a low-skilled one. The expected payoffs of innovative and non-innovative firms are given by,

[25]Note that $0<\frac{CE-(\bar{s}-s)}{(\bar{p}-p)}<1$ holds.

$$E(I) = \text{prob}(S)\left[B_I(S) - B_I(NS) - (\bar{s} + \bar{p}) + (s + p)\right] + B_I(NS) - (s + p + CI)$$
$$E(NI) = \text{prob}(S)\left[B_{NI}(S) - B_{NI}(NS) - \bar{s} + s\right] + B_{NI}(NS) - s$$

Hence, a firm prefers to be innovative if and only if the expected payoff of being innovative is greater than the expected payoff of being non-innovative, i.e., $E(I) > E(NI)$ or,

$$\text{prob}(S) > \frac{B_I(NS) - B_{NI}(NS) - p - CI}{B_I(NS) - B_I(S) + B_{NI}(S) - B_{NI}(NS) + (\bar{p} - p)}. \quad (5.5)$$

Let us call $\text{prob}(I) = P_u$ and $\text{prob}(S) = \bar{x}_s$. Hence, the threshold level where both firms and workers prefer to be high-profile is $(\bar{x}_s, P_u)$. Therefore, the game has three Nash equilibria. Two in pure strategies: $A = \{S, I\}$ and $B = \{NS, NI\}$ and a mixed strategy Nash equilibrium given by:

$$NE = (\bar{x}_s, (1 - \bar{x}_s);\ P_u, (1 - P_u)),$$

where it follows that equilibrium A Pareto-dominates equilibrium B, while B is the risk dominant equilibrium.

In the following sections, we study the dynamic complementarities for the types of firms and workers. We consider the workers' population dynamic, and from such population dynamics, we characterize the dynamic equilibria and we find the threshold value to overcome the low level equilibrium. Moreover, we consider the dynamics of the firms with labor inputs.

5.2. Dynamic Imitation of Workers

Hereafter, we consider the populations of firms and workers normalized to a measure of 1. Hence, $\text{prob}(I) = PI = QI / Q$ where QI is the number of innovative firms, and Q is the total number of firms. Then, $\text{prob}(NI) = PNI = 1 - PI$.

Consider that a potential worker may assess whether or not to change her current behavior. Let R_i be the probability that the $i-$ strategist, $i \in \{S, NS\}$, raises the question about whether she must change her current behavior or not. Then, R_i denotes the average time-rate at which an individual worker, currently using strategy $i \in \{S, NS\}$, reviews her strategy choice.

Let P_{ij} be the probability that the reviewing worker will really change to the strategy $j \neq i$. Then,

$$P(i \to j) = R_i P_{ij}, \qquad (5.6)$$

is the probability that a worker of the $i-th$ club changes to the $j-th$ club. In the following, $e_S = (1,0)$ and $e_{NS} = (0,1)$ indicate the vector of pure strategies, S or NS.

Hence, the percentage of the expected flow of high-skilled workers, $\dot{X}_S$, will be equal to the percent probability of the low-skilled changing to a high-skilled worker's club minus the percent probability of the high-skilled changing to a low-skilled worker's club. Since we consider large populations, we invoke the law of large numbers and model these aggregate stochastic processes as deterministic flows, with each flow being set equal to the expected rate of the corresponding Poisson arrival process. Rearranging terms, we get the system of differential equations that characterizes the dynamic flow of workers,

$$\begin{aligned} \dot{X}_S &= R_{NS} P_{NSS} X_{NS} - R_S P_{SNS} X_S \\ \dot{X}_{NS} &= -\dot{X}_S \end{aligned} \qquad (5.7)$$

where X_S is the fraction of high-skilled workers and X_{NS} is the fraction of low-skilled workers.

Let us state the following definition about imitative population dynamics.

> Definition 21. *A population dynamic (5.7) will be called "imitative" if there are at least two different strategies, and an agent following one of these strategies assesses, with a given probability, whether he must change his own behavior or not, and the final decision depends on the relation between the benefits he obtains and the benefits others obtain by following a different behavior.*

An imitative dynamic, as defined by the equation system (5.7), makes sense if there are at least two different behaviors, one of them currently followed and the other as a possible behavior to imitate. In this model, if one of the two kinds of populations disappears, there is no incentive to change.

We consider that reviewing workers evaluate their current strategy and they decide to imitate successful strategies. Assume that potential workers do not observe payoffs of individual neighbors, but they can, in some way, compute average payoffs in their neighborhoods and they imitate the behavior that leads to the highest average payoff.

Although the worker does not know all the true values of the payoff of the other workers, she can take a sample of true values to estimate the average. Let $\widetilde{E}(i)$ and $\widetilde{E}(j)$ be the estimators of those true values $E(i)$ and $E(j)$. Hence, each $i-$worker changes her current strategy if and only if $\widetilde{E}(i) < \widetilde{E}(j)$.

Consider that the probability of an $i-$ type strategist becoming a $j-$type strategist is given by

$P[\widetilde{E}(j) - \widetilde{E}(i) > 0]$,

and thus (5.7) can be written as,

$$\dot{X}_S = R_{NS} P[\widetilde{E}(NS) - \widetilde{E}(S) < 0] X_{NS} - R_S P[\widetilde{E}(NS) - \widetilde{E}(S) > 0] X_S, \qquad (5.8)$$

$$\dot{X}_{NS} = -\dot{X}_S.$$

Consider that the value $P[\widetilde{E}(j) - \widetilde{E}(i) > 0]$ increases proportionally to the true value $E(j)$ if $E(j) > 0$. This probability is equal to zero if $E(j) < 0$, i.e. $\forall \; i, j \in \{S, NS\}$, i.e.:

$$P[\widetilde{E}(j) > \widetilde{E}(i)] = \begin{cases} \lambda E(j) & \text{if } \; E(j) > 0 \\ \\ 0 & \text{if } \; E(j) < 0 \end{cases} \qquad (5.9)$$

where $\lambda = \frac{1}{|E(NS)+E(S)|}$.[26]

Let us assume a constant number of innovative firms, PI; and that salaries $(\bar{s}, s)$, premiums $(\bar{p}, p)$, and education costs CE are fixed or

---

[26] If $E(j) < 0$, then $P\left[\widetilde{E}(j) > \widetilde{E}(i)\right] = 0$ and then it can be that the complementary probability $P\left[\widetilde{E}(j) < \widetilde{E}(i)\right] = 1$, otherwise this complementary probability is not well defined. Hence, $\lambda E(j) \in (0,1]$.

given in the economy. Then, $E(S)$ and $E(NS)$ are constant.

Recall that $E(NS)=(PI)(p)+s\geq 0$ while $E(S)=(PI)(\overline{p})+\overline{s}-CE$ can be either positive or negative, depending on the values PI and CE. Given salaries and prizes, if CE is fixed, then $E(S)>0$ if and only if $PI>\frac{CE-\overline{s}}{\overline{p}}$. Let us denote by,

$$\pi=\frac{CE-\overline{s}}{\overline{p}} \tag{5.10}$$

the percentage of innovative firms, such that $E(S) = 0$.

In this way, the system (5.8) can take one of the following forms:

If $E(S) < 0$**,** then $P\left[\widetilde{E}(S)-\widetilde{E}(NS)>0\right]=0$.[27] The evolution of the high-skilled workers is given by the dynamical system,

$$\dot{X}_S=-R_S\lambda E(NS)X_S.$$

Its solution is,

$$X_S(t)=X_S(0)\exp\left(\frac{-R_SE(NS)}{|E(NS)+E(S)|}\right)t$$

where $X_S(0)$ is the fraction of the high-skill workers at time $t=0$.[28] The population of high-skilled workers decreases. The only possibility of changing this situation is to increase the premia of high-skilled workers or to reduce education costs. Therefore, the population of high-skilled workers decreases and vanishes. But, this trend can be modified by changing the parameters of the model, which is a necessary condition. A policy maker can implement a policy to reduce training costs (education costs) and to increase the prizes given to high-skilled workers.

If $E(S) > 0$, then the dynamical system takes the form,

---

[27] Note that the complementarity probability $P\left[E(NS)>E(S)\right]=\frac{E(NS)}{|E(S)+E(NS)|}\in(0,1]$ is well defined.

[28] Indeed, when $P\left[E(NS)>E(S)\right]=\frac{E(NS)}{|E(S)+E(NS)|}=1$, and the expression (5.12) should be $X_S(t)=X_S(0)\exp\left(-R_St\right)$.

$$\dot{X}_S = -[R_{NS}E(S) + R_S E(NS)]\lambda X_S + R_{NS}\lambda E(S).$$
$$\dot{X}_{NS} = -\dot{X}_S. \tag{5.13}$$

Let us label $A = \lambda[R_{NS}E(S) + R_S E(NS)]$ and $B = R_{NS}\lambda E(S)$. Then the solution of the differential equation (eq:sdis) in this case is,

$$X_S(t) = \left(X_S(0) - \frac{B}{A} \right)\exp(-At) + \frac{B}{A}. \tag{5.14}$$

where $X_S(0)$ is the fraction of high-skilled workers at time $t = 0$ and,
$$\frac{B}{A} = \frac{R_{NS}E(S)}{R_{NS}E(S) + R_S E(NS)}.$$

Note that the percentage of high-skilled workers converge to $\frac{B}{A}$. By substitution of expected payoffs, $E(\cdot)$, we get,

$$\frac{B}{A} = \frac{R_{NS}[(PI)(\bar{p}) + \bar{s} - CE]}{R_{NS}[(PI)(\bar{p}) + \bar{s} - CE] + R_S[(PI)(p) + s]}.$$

This value depends on the initially given percentage of innovative firms, and increases with this percentage. Considering the percentage B/A as a function of the initial percentage of innovative firms PI, it follows that this value increases with PI. Note that even in the case of a country where all firms are innovative, i.e., $PI = 1$, it does not follow that at the limit, all workers will become high-skilled. In this case, at the equilibrium, the percentage of high-skilled workers is given by:

$$B/A = \frac{R_{NS}[\bar{p} + \bar{s} - CE]}{R_{NS}[\bar{p} + \bar{s} - CE] + R_S[p + s]}.$$

A particularly interesting case occurs where $PI = P_u = \frac{CE-(\bar{s}-s)}{(\bar{p}-p)}$. In this case, the percentage of innovative firms is equal to the value where workers are indifferent about being high-skilled or low-skilled. Given that $P_u > \pi$, the economy evolves to a high level equilibrium, where

$$\frac{B}{A} = \frac{R_{NS}}{R_{NS} + R_S}.$$

is the limit of the percentage of high-skilled workers.

Provided that $E(NS) > 0$ (i.e., strictly positive), the results, although intuitive, depend completely on the fact that $E(S)$ can be negative, while $E(NS)$ can only be strictly positive. In simple words, while the probability of transitioning from low-skilled to high-skilled can be zero, the reverse is not possible (the transition from high-skilled to low-skilled cannot be zero). The assumptions are such that an all-skilled state is not even a stationary state.

5.3. Initial Conditions Matter

How does the initial number of innovative firms PI explain the economy's evolution path? Consider two countries, 1 and 2, where the respective percentages of innovative firms in $t = t_0$ are given by $PI_1 > PI_2$. So, looking at the solution of (5.13), it follows that the population of high-skilled workers in country 1 is, for each $t > t_0$, larger than the population of high-skilled workers in country 2, i.e.,

$$X_{1S}(t) > X_{2S}(t), \ \forall t > t_0$$

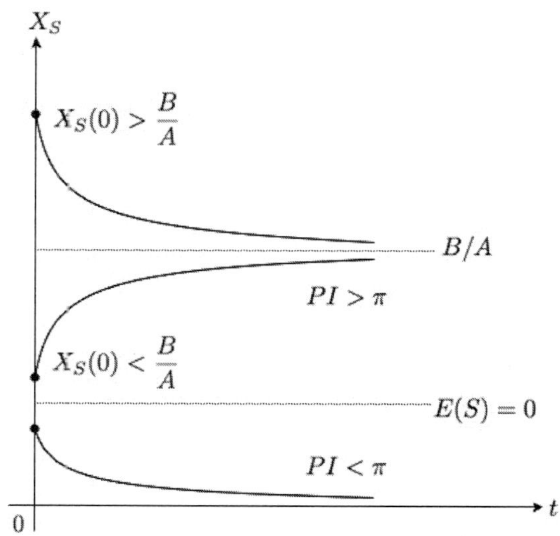

Figure 5-1. Convergence of high-skilled workers: above and below the threshold value.

So, the equilibrium state is higher in country 1 than in country 2, which means that the number of high-skilled workers in equilibrium is higher in the first country than in the second. Now, recall the threshold dynamic value, π, of the number of innovative firms corresponding to $E(S)=0$, i.e. $\pi=\frac{CE-\bar{s}}{\bar{p}}$, such that as described in Figure 5-1, we get that:

1) If $PI>\pi$ then:
   a) if $X_S(0)>\frac{B}{A}$, the population of high-skilled workers is decreasing and converges to $\frac{B}{A}$,
   b) if $X_S(0)<\frac{B}{A}$, the population of high-skilled workers is increasing and converges to $\frac{B}{A}$.
   c) In both cases, the economy converges to the high level equilibrium.
2) If $PI<\pi$ then:
   The population of high-skilled workers is decreasing over time to 0, and the economy is in a poverty trap, since it is the rational behavior of workers to be low-skilled, and for firms to decide to be non-innovative.

The following theorem summarizes our results.

Theorem. *Consider the imitative dynamics, given by the system (5.7). There exists a threshold value,* $\pi=\frac{CE-\bar{s}}{\bar{p}}$, *such that*

1. *If the initial number of innovative firms* PI *is larger than this value, i.e.,* $PI>\pi$, *then the percentage of high-skilled workers* $X_S(t)$ *converges to* $\frac{B}{A}$.
2. *If the initial number of innovative firms* PI *verify,* $PI<\pi$, *then the percentage of high-skilled workers* $X_S(t)$ *converges to 0.*

Proof. **Case 1**. If $PI>\pi$, then $E(S)>0$ and the evolution of the population follows the dynamical system (5.13). So, the population of high-skilled workers is given by $X_S(t)=X_S(0)e^{-At}+\frac{B}{A}$ and $X_S(t)\rightarrow\frac{B}{A}$.
Case 2. If $PI<\pi$, then $E(S)\leq 0$ and the evolution of the population of high-skilled workers follows the evolution given by (eq:dynsysle), so the population of high-skilled workers is decreasing to zero. We can conclude from this theorem that if $\pi<PI\leq 1$, then in the long-run, the percentage of high-skilled workers in the economy will be $\frac{B}{A}$. It follows that non-innovative firms coexist with innovative firms and a percentage of high-

skilled workers, that at the limit is equal to $\frac{B}{A}$, coexists with a group of low-skilled workers. However, if $PI < \pi$, the economy is in a poverty trap and the corresponding stable equilibrium $(0,1;0,1)$ is a Nash equilibrium.

Furthermore, let us introduce an index of the location of the economy; that is,

$$U = \frac{PI}{\pi}. \tag{5.15}$$

Then, if $U \leq 1$, then the economy is in a poverty trap, i.e., it converges to the low equilibrium where all workers are low-skilled and all firms are non-innovative. If $U > 1$, then the economy has overcome the poverty trap, and it converges to a high level equilibrium.

Hence, an economy can be located either in a poverty trap or a high-level equilibrium, depending on the relationship between the number of innovative firms and the parameters (training costs and premia) of the model, this relation is summarized by the index U.

In our setup, an institutional policy that increases the value of U tends to shrink the basin of attraction of the low stationary state. A change in the parameters of the model, reducing education costs or increasing rewards for skill workers, may drive the economy out of the basin of attraction of the low state.

5.4. Dynamic Equilibria and Nash Equilibria

In our set up, there is no possibility of observing the high Nash equilibrium (in pure strategies) $(S,I) = (1,0;1,0)$ because it is not a dynamic equilibrium. On the contrary, the low Nash equilibrium $(NS,NI) = (0,1;0,1)$ is an asymptotically stable equilibrium, and the poverty trap arises because of rational behavior by the agents. A worker's rational choice is to imitate the best performing strategy (in this case to become the $NS-$type). A firm's rational choice is not to invest in an R&D department or not to innovate when the initial number of innovative firms PI is below the threshold value π.

We observe a specific possible mixed Nash equilibrium given by,

$$NE = (\bar{x}_s, (1-\bar{x}_s);\ P_u, (1-P_u)),$$

such that, given the distribution of the firms $(P_u, (1-P_u))$, the equality

$E(S) = E(NS)$ is verified. And, given the distribution of the workers' population $(\bar{x}_s, (1-\bar{x}_s))$, the firms are indifferent between being innovative or not being innovative i.e., $E(I) = E(NI)$. Hence, in the mixed Nash equilibrium, since the number of innovative firms is $PI = P_u = \frac{CE-(\bar{s}-s)}{(\bar{p}-p)} > \pi$, the population of high-skilled workers converges to $\frac{B}{A} = \frac{R_{NS}}{R_{NS}+R_S}$ which can be equal to $\bar{x}_s$ for the specific case in which the average time-rate at which an individual worker reviews her strategy choice, R_i $\forall i \in \{S, NS\}$, is defined such that $\frac{R_{NS}}{R_{NS}+R_S} = \bar{x}_s$.

Let us now consider the concept of an *evolutionarily stable strategy against the field* given a profile distribution of the firm's population, y. Let Δ^w be the set of distributions of the workers population, and let Δ^F be the set of distributions of the firms. Let $x_w = (x_s, x_{ns}) \in \Delta^w$ be a population distribution of workers and let $y_f = (y, 1-y) \in \Delta^F$ be a population distribution of firms.

Consider a perturbation in the distribution of the firms and let y_ε be the post-perturbation distribution. Let $\varepsilon > 0$ be sufficiently small, such that the Euclidean distance $| y_f - y_\varepsilon | < \varepsilon$.

Definition 22. *We say that $x_w \in \Delta^w$ is an evolutionarily stable strategy (ESS) against the field given by y_f, if*

1) *The expected value $E(x_w / y_f) > E(x'_w / y_f)$ for all $x'_w \neq x_w \in \Delta^w$, and*
2) *$E(x_w / y_\varepsilon) > E(x'_w / y_\varepsilon)$ for all $x'_w \neq x_w \in \Delta^w$.*

Intuitively, this means that: (i) x_w is the only best response against y_f, and (ii) this distribution does better against perturbations (in the distributions of the *field*) than all other distributions. In our case, when $y \leq \pi$ the distribution $x_w = (0,1)$ – all workers are low-skilled – is an ESS against the field given by y_f.

We can study the dynamics of the firms – whether they innovate or not – supported by the hypothesis of "Skill-Biased Technical Change". Recent studies develop different models to prove that high-skilled labor and high-technology firms are complements in order to obtain a high-level equilibrium (particularly, see Acemoglu, 1997; 1998). This is the well-known notion of skill-biased technical change. Skill-biased technical change implies a shift in the production technology that favors high-skilled over low-skilled labor by increasing the relative productivity of high-skilled labor and, therefore, its relative demand (see Acemoglu, 2002; Aghion, 2006; Hornstein et al., 2005).

To analyze strategic complementarities, let us suppose that innovative firms are represented by the technological production function,

$$y = f(z, x_s, x_{ns}) \tag{5.16}$$

where z is the technology, x_s the number of high-skilled workers and x_{ns} the number of low-skilled workers engaged by the firm, and y the product obtained by the firm from these inputs.

We assume that R&D technology is a complementary input to high-skilled labor.[29] Hence the marginal product of the technology is an increasing function of the number of high-skilled workers. Let $x_s(t)$ be the total number of high-skilled workers hired by innovative firms at the time t. Consider the time $t_0 < t_1$ and suppose that the number of high-skilled workers is increasing with time, i.e. $x_s(t_0) < x_s(t_1)$. Then, from the hypothesis about technology, it follows that,

$$\frac{\partial c(y, x_s(t_1))}{\partial y} \leq \frac{\partial c(y, x_s(t_0))}{\partial y}, \tag{5.17}$$

where $c(y, x_s)$ denotes the short run cost function. Hence, there exists $\bar{y}$, such that $c(y, x_s(t_0)) > c(y, x_s(t_1))\,; \forall y > \bar{y}$. Figure 5-2 draws a graphical representation.

[29]For instance $y = z^{\alpha} x_s^{\beta} + x_{ns}$ where $0 < \alpha, \beta < 1$.

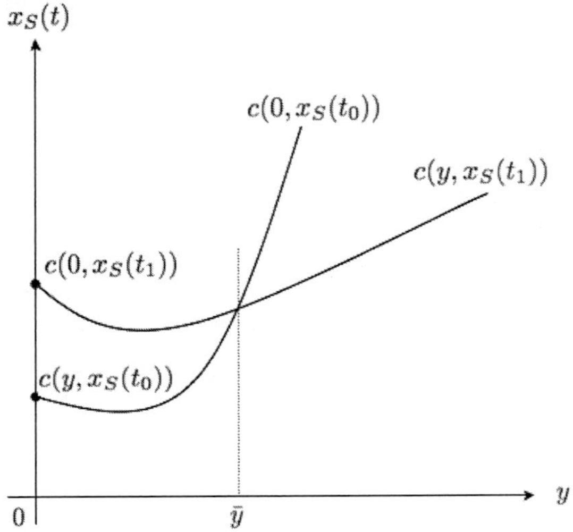

Figure 5-2. Decreasing marginal costs for the innovative firms.

Thus, if the number of high-skilled workers is increasing, the cost of innovative firms decreases in the long-run. The innovative firms can obtain positive profits, and they therefore have incentives to enter an industry. Non-innovative firms, with negative profits in the long-run, wish to exit the industry. The following reason reinforces this conclusion about the evolution of the firms: *Innovative firms require high-skilled workers, whereas non-innovative firms require low-skilled workers*, but the number of low-skilled workers decreases when the number of innovative firms is sufficiently high. Hence, the demand for low-skilled workers will be lower when innovation appears. Hence, a positive net flux of low-skilled to high-skilled workers should be observed as a consequence of an accelerating process of innovation and, at the same time, this process is enhanced by the existence of an increasing demand for high-skilled labor.

To understand the situation described above, let us consider the following case. Suppose that the firms are characterized by the technological function:

$$f(z, x_s, x_{ns}) = kz^{\alpha} x_s^{\beta} + x_{ns}^{\lambda}.$$

Where:

$$k = \begin{cases} H & \text{if the firm is innovative} \\ h & \text{if the firm is non-innovative,} \end{cases}$$

$H > h > 0$, and α, β and λ are positive constants such that $\alpha + \beta = 1$ and $\lambda < 1$.

Assume that the feasible technology $z = \bar{z}$ is a given positive constant, and that skill premia (the bonus of being a high-skilled worker) are denoted by pr. The short run cost function is therefore:

$$C(x_{ns}, y, \bar{z}, \bar{x}_s) = (w_s + pr)x_s + w_{ns}\left[y - k\bar{z}^{\alpha} x_s^{\beta}\right]^{\frac{1}{\lambda}}. \tag{5.18}$$

It follows that:

$$C_y'(x_{ns}, y, \bar{z}, \bar{x}_s) = w_{ns}\,\tfrac{1}{\lambda}\left[y - k\bar{z}^{\alpha} x_s^{\beta}\right]^{\frac{1}{\lambda}-1}.$$

$$C_{y,x_{ns}}''(x_{ns}, y, \bar{z}, \bar{x}_s) = -w_{ns}\left(\tfrac{1}{\lambda} - 1\right)\tfrac{1}{\lambda}\left[y - k\bar{z}^{\alpha} x_s^{\beta}\right]^{\frac{1}{\lambda}-2} k\bar{z}^{\alpha} x_s^{\beta-1} < 0.$$

Thus, for the case of innovative firms, it can be observed that the marginal cost decreases with x_s faster than in the case of non-innovative firms. So if in $t = t_0$, the fraction of innovative firms is greater than the threshold value $\bar{\pi}$, then innovative firms can reduce their costs more quickly than non-innovative firms.

Assume that the market price for the product is p. If we assume that firms are competitive, then the optimal supply for each firm is given by:

$$Y_I^* = pHz^{\alpha} x_{Is}^* + x_{Ins}^*$$

$$Y_{NI}^* = phz^{\alpha} x_{NIs}^* + x_{NIns}^*$$

Where x_{is}^* and x_{ins}^*, $i \in \{I, NI\}$ denote the long run demand for inputs for innovative and non-innovative firms:

$$x_{Ins}^* = x_{NIns}^* = \left(\frac{w_{ns}}{\lambda p}\right)^{\frac{1}{\beta-1}}, \; x_{Is}^* = \left(\frac{w_s + pr}{\lambda pHz^{\alpha}\beta}\right)^{\frac{1}{\beta-1}}, \; x_{NIs}^* = \left(\frac{w_s + pr'}{\lambda phz^{\alpha}\beta}\right)^{\frac{1}{\beta-1}}.$$

Let $PI > \pi$ be the existing number of innovative firms in time $t = t_0$ and let $D(p)$ be the demand of the market for the product. The total supply $S(p)$ of the innovative firms will be equal to:

$$S(p) = (PI)Y_I^*.$$

The number of non-innovative firms will be equal to:

$$\max\left\{\frac{D(p)-S(p)}{Y^*_{NI}},0\right\}.$$

Therefore, in the long run, a percentage of innovative firms could coexist with a percentage of non-innovative firms. To see this, assume that there is an associated cost to becoming an innovative firm (the investment cost of R&D departments), and let $C(h,H)$ be this cost. So, an incumbent non-innovative firm has an incentive to become an innovative firm if and only if the benefits are such that:

$$B(NI) < B(I) - C(h,H).$$

This possibility depends on, among other things, the segment of the market that the firm can obtain given the existing number of innovative firms in the market. When $B(I) - C(h,H) < B(NI)$, the firm prefers to continue being non-innovative.

Consider that firms' decisions to innovate or not to innovate depend on a given number of high-skilled workers and on the investment costs of innovation. Recall that a firm decides to be innovative if and only if $E(I) > E(NI)$ like equation (5.5), i.e.

$$x_S > \frac{B_I(NS) - B_{NI}(NS) - p - CI}{B_I(NS) - B_I(S) + B_{NI}(S) - B_{NI}(NS) + (\bar{p} - p)}.$$

where x_S is the share of high-skilled workers. Nevertheless, the behavioral rule that firms should use to decide be innovative or not should consider both: i) the cost of investment, denoted by CI, and, ii) the number of high-skilled workers who make such an investment profitable in the long-run. It is the threshold dynamic value corresponding to $E(S)=0$ or $\pi = \frac{CS-\bar{s}}{p}$. Therefore, the investment in innovation is profitable when:

$$\pi - CI > 0.$$

Let us normalize the firms' population to 1, $y_I + y_{NI} = 1$. As before, let R_{ij} be the probability that the $i-$ strategist, $i \in \{I, NI\}$, raises the question about whether or not she must change her current behavior to $j \neq i \in \{I, NI\}$. Hence, the dynamic flow of firms is given by,

$$\dot{Y}_I = R_{NII}(\pi - CI)E(I)(1-Y_I) - R_{INI}(\pi - CI)E(NI)Y_I$$

$$\dot{Y}_{NI} = -\dot{Y}_I$$

Rearranging the terms, we get:

$$\dot{Y}_I = R_{NII}(\pi - CI)E(I) - Y_I\left[R_{NII}(\pi - CI)E(I) + R_{INI}(\pi - CI)E(NI)\right]$$

Let us label

$$f = R_{NII}(\pi - CI)E(I)$$

and

$$g = \left[R_{NII}(\pi - CI)E(I) + R_{INI}(\pi - CI)E(NI)\right]$$

Then, the solution to $\dot{Y}_I$ is:

$$Y_I(t) = \left(Y_I(0) - \frac{f}{g}\right)\exp(-gt) + \frac{f}{g},$$

where:

$$\frac{f}{g} = \frac{R_{NII}E(I)}{R_{NII}E(I) + R_{INII}E(NI)},$$

is interpreted as: **the ratio of coexisting innovative and non innovative firms that review their strategies, given a certain initial number of high-skilled workers x_s in the economy.**

Recall that the expected payoffs of innovative $E(I)$ and non innovative firms $E(NI)$ are defined as a function of x_s and $E(I)?0$ if:

$$x_s \geq \frac{B_I(NS) - p - s - CI}{B_I(NS) - B_I(S) + \overline{p} + \overline{s} - p - s}.$$

Figure 5-3 draws the evolution of firms given a threshold x_s.

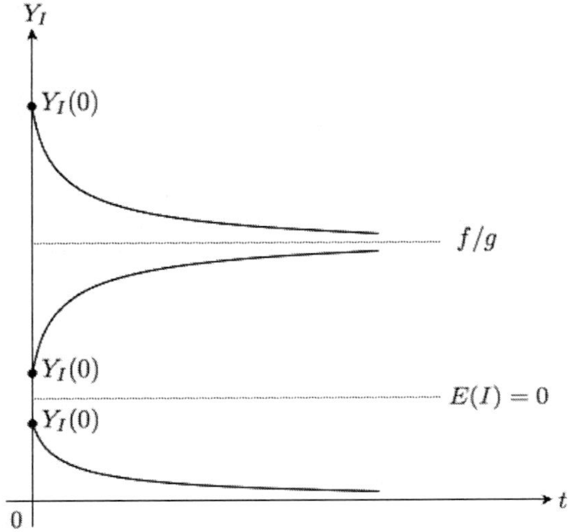

Figure 5-3. Dynamic evolution of firms from above and below the threshold level.

5.5. Concluding Remarks

We have presented a game theoretical model concerning the strategic complementarities between different types of firms and workers. Workers follow an imitative behavior and firms decide to invest or not in R&D depending on the current number of high-skilled labor in the economy.

We conclude that to overcome a poverty trap, it is necessary to surpass a threshold number of innovative firms. Once this threshold is reached, workers will have an incentive to improve their skills. Firms, in turn, can obtain more benefits by investing in R&D. The main problem in overcoming a poverty trap is that all the agents involved act rationally, but the rational persistence of a poverty trap is inefficient. As we have shown, a threshold value from which the rationality changes exists; that is to say, to invoke a coordination problem. Thus, above such a threshold, the agents are able to coordinate to the high level equilibrium. And surpassing this value, the agents rationally change their behavior and the economy moves to another, Pareto superior, equilibrium. Since there exists a continuum of possible high equilibria, one for each percentage of innovative firms between the threshold value π and 1, there exists a continuum of countries in high equilibria but with different percentages of innovative firms and high-skilled workers.

A policy maker in a developed country, i.e. a country with a high level equilibrium, who wishes to improve their level of equilibrium or needs to improve the efficiency of the industry, may do this by designing a mechanism to transform the industry, say by favoring the substitution of non-innovative firms for innovative firms. A benevolent policy maker in an under developed country faces two options to overcome the poverty trap, either 1) to improve the efficiency of the industry favoring the substitution of non-innovative firms for innovative firms, or 2) to adopt a policy that decreases the threshold values given by π, in such way that new trajectories belong to the basin of attraction of a high equilibrium. This objective may be attained by reducing the training costs to become a high-skilled worker, or giving incentives to innovative firms to increase the rewards for high-skilled workers. From our model, it can be seen that the closer a country gets to the technology threshold, the more that investment in education enhances growth.

In summary, policy makers should find the right mechanism to allow agents to choose the most efficient behavior. Differences in the policies followed by institutions in different countries can help us to understand differences in the degree of development across countries and over time. A fundamental and enduring concern of a policy maker is the design of an incentive policy that is conducive to increasing the number of innovative firms and the possibility of workers becoming highly skilled.

For further research, intuitively, by a suitable modification of the probability of changing (expression x), a model of imitation based on the difference of expected payoffs could have (at least) three sets of *stationary states*: all high-skilled, all low-skilled, and a mixed one. Moreover, the intuition says that the all high-skilled state should not be *asymptotically stable*, and the results, at the end, should be similar to those found in this paper. Another possibility is to keep expression x, avoiding strictly negative expected payoffs (i.e., assume $E(S) > 0$ and $E(NS) > 0$). In this case, we would always have a mixed equilibrium, which would depend, among other things, on the relative rates of change (R_S and R_{NS}).

CHAPTER SIX

THE REPLICATOR DYNAMICS FOR FIRMS AND WORKERS

Consider the imitative behavior of both agents, i.e. both firms and workers (see Accinelli and Sanchez Carrera, 2011). Therefore, we present an imitation game where the nature of interactions among agents creates a potential for multiple equilibria. We find the replicator dynamic system and the ESSs. Moreover, we show how an economy may move beyond the poverty trap by 'playing against the field'. That is, when the economy is already in the basin of attraction of the low-level equilibrium, then the agents play against such a state of the economy by imitating the high-profile economic agents. An economy in the basin of attraction of a poverty trap can be improved by exogenous changes or by external interventions. Moreover, we study the replicator dynamic with payoff taxation as the way in which a policymaker can make interventions in the economy to encourage firms and workers to be of high-profile, and then to overcome the poverty trap.

6.1. The Replicator by Imitation

Consider that in each period of time $t \in [0,\infty)$, an agent from each population is randomly matched with an agent from another population to play a bilateral finite game. Recall that $\text{prob}(I) = PI = y_I$ is the worker's probability of being hired by an innovative firm, and $\text{prob}(S) = x_S$ is the firm's probability of hiring a high-skilled worker.

Let N_i^τ be the total of $i-$ strategists, $i \in \{(I,NI);(S,NS)\}$, from the total population, $\tau \in \{F,W\}$, and both populations are normalized to 1, that is, $y_I + y_{NI} = 1$ and $x_S + x_{NS} = 1$.

Hence, the fractions of $S-$type strategists and $I-$type strategist are,

$$x_S = \frac{N_S^W}{N_S^W + N_{NS}^W},$$

$$y_I = \frac{N_I^F}{N_I^F + N_{NI}^F}.$$

In the following, the vectors $y_F = (y_I, y_{NI})$ and $x_W = (x_S, x_{NS})$ are distributions of agents playing a certain pure or mixed strategy in the space $\{(I, NI);(S, NS)\}$ from the two populations F and W.

Now, the expected payoffs are[30]:

$$\begin{cases} E(S) = y_I \bar{p} + \bar{s} - CE. \\ E(NS) = y_I p + s. \\ E(I) = x_S \left[B_I(S) - B_I(NS) - (\bar{s} + \bar{p}) + (s + p)\right] + B_I(NS) - (s + p + CI). \\ E(NI) = x_S \left[B_{NI}(S) - B_{NI}(NS) - \bar{s} + s\right] + B_{NI}(NS) - s. \end{cases} \tag{6.1}$$

6.1.1 The Specific Behavioral Rule

Let us consider the definition of the **Behavioral Rule**. The *outflow* from club i in population τ is $q_i^\tau r_i^\tau(x) p_{ij}^\tau(x)$ and the *inflow* is $q_j^\tau r_j^\tau(x) p_{ji}^\tau(x)$, where $q_i^\tau = q^\tau x_i^\tau$ is the number of *i*-strategist agents from population τ and q^τ represents the whole population τ, hence $q^\tau = q_i^\tau + q_j^\tau$. Hence, for population τ (assuming that the size of the population τ is constant), by the law of large numbers, we can model these processes as a deterministic flow. Rearranging the terms, for each pair $i, j \in \{(I, NI);(S, NS)\}$, $j \neq i$, from population $\tau \in \{F, W\}$, we get,

$$\dot{x}_i^\tau = r_j^\tau(x) p_{ji}^\tau(x) x_j^\tau - r_i^\tau(x) p_{ij}^\tau(x) x_i^\tau. \tag{6.2}$$

[30]Recall that $E(NS) = y_I p + s$ is always positive, but $E(S) = y_I \bar{p} + \bar{s} - CE$ can be positive or negative depending on y_I and CE. We interpreted $E(S) < 0$ as the case in which the probability of being hired by an innovative firm tends to zero, and then the cost of education is greater than salaries, i.e., $\lim_{\phi_I \to 0} E(S) < 0$ if $CE > \bar{s}$.

Consider that the an agent's decision depends upon the expected payoff associated with his or her own behavior, given the composition of the other population, $E^{\tau}(e_i,x^{-\tau})$ (where τ represents the population to which the agent following the *i-th* behavior belongs, and $-\tau \in \{F,W\}$, $-\tau \neq \tau$), and also depends on the characteristics of the populations represented by $x=(y^f,x^W)$. We may therefore assume,

$$r_i^{\tau}(x)=f_i^{\tau}(E^{\tau}(e_i,x^{-\tau}),x). \tag{6.3}$$

Function $f_i^{\tau}(E^{\tau}(e_i,x^{-\tau}),x)$ is interpreted as the propensity of a member from the i -th club to switch membership as a function of the expected utility gains from such a switch. Agents with less successful strategies on average review their strategy at a higher rate than agents with more successful strategies. Assume f_i^{τ} is population-specific, but the same across all its components, independent of club membership, and assume, furthermore, that it is linear in utility levels (see Weibull, 1995). Thus, the propensity to switch behavior will be decreasing in the level of utility,i.e.,

$$f_i^{\tau}(E^{\tau}(e_i,x^{-\tau}))=\alpha^{\tau}-\boldsymbol{\beta}^{\tau}E^{\tau}(e_i,x^{-\tau})\in[0,1]. \tag{6.4}$$

where $\alpha^{\tau},\beta^{\tau}\geq 0$ and $\frac{\alpha^{\tau}}{\beta^{\tau}}\geq E^{\tau}(e_i,x^{-\tau})$.

To simplify the notation, for each pair $i,j\in\{(I,NI);(S,NS)\}$, $j\neq i$ let us simply label:

- $r_i^{\tau}(x)=r_i$ and $r_j^{\tau}(x)=r_j$,
- $p_{ji}^{\tau}(x)=p_{ji}$ and $p_{ij}^{\tau}(x)=p_{ij}$,
- $E^{\tau}(e_i,x^{-\tau})=E(i)$ and $E^{\tau}(e_j,x^{-\tau})=E(j)$.

In particular, if we consider the profile distribution of workers, $x_W=(x_S,x_{NS})$, and firms, $y_F=(y_I,y_{NI})$, then we can model the flow of high-skilled workers and innovative firms over time: $\dot{x}_S$ and $\dot{y}_I$.

Since we consider large populations, we invoke the law of large numbers and model these aggregate stochastic processes as deterministic flows, each such flow being set equal to the expected rate of the corresponding Poisson arrival process. Hence, rearranging terms, we obtain the system of differential equations that characterize the dynamic flow of workers,

$$\begin{aligned} \dot{x}_S &= r_{NS} p_{NSS} x_{NS} - r_S p_{SNS} x_S \\ \dot{x}_{NS} &= -\dot{x}_S \end{aligned} \tag{6.5}$$

and the differential equations that characterize the dynamic flow of firms,

$$\begin{aligned} \dot{y}_I &= r_{NI} p_{NII} y_{NI} - r_I p_{INI} y_I \\ \dot{y}_{NI} &= -\dot{y}_I \end{aligned} \tag{6.6}$$

An agent does not know the true values of the expected payoffs that other agents receive, but she can take a sample of such true values in order to estimate the average. Let $\widetilde{E}(i)$ and $\widetilde{E}(j)$ be the estimators for the true values $E(i)$ and $E(j)$, $\forall i, j \in \{(I, NI); (S, NS)\}$, $j \neq i$. Hence, each $i-$ strategist changes her current strategy if and only if $P[\widetilde{E}(i) < \widetilde{E}(j)]$.

From Chapter 3, we apply the **Specific Behavioral Rule** where a reviewing worker, i, who decides to change her current strategy must take into consideration both the probability of imitating at least one strategy that performs better than her current strategy, $P[\widetilde{E}(i) < \widetilde{E}(j)]$, and the probability of meeting an agent, x_j^τ, who uses such a strategy, i.e. a reviewing strategist *i* changes to *j* with a probability, p_{ij}, equal to getting a positive average rule times the probability of finding a *j*-strategist in the whole population, i.e. $p_{ij} = P[\widetilde{E}(j) - \widetilde{E}(i) > 0]x_j$, where $P[\widetilde{E}(j) - \widetilde{E}(i) > 0]$ increases proportionally to the true value $E(j)$, i.e. $\forall i, j \in \{(I, NI); (S, NS)\}$, $j \neq i$:

$$P[\widetilde{E}(j) > \widetilde{E}(i)]x_j^\tau = \begin{cases} \lambda E(j) x_j^\tau & if \;\; E(j) > 0 \\ 0 & if \;\; E(j) \leq 0 \end{cases} \tag{6.7}$$

where $\lambda = \frac{1}{|E(i) + E(j)|}$.

From equations (6.3, 6.4 and 6.7), and after some algebraic manipulations, system (6.2) becomes the replicator dynamic driven by imitation, i.e.,

$$\dot{x}_i^\tau = x_i^\tau\left(1 - x_i^\tau\right)\left[\lambda\left(\alpha^\tau + \boldsymbol{\beta}^\tau\right)\left(E(i) - E(j)\right)\right] \tag{6.8}$$

where $x_i^\tau \in [0,1]$ and $\dot{x}_i^\tau + \dot{x}_j^\tau = 0$ from population $\tau \in \{F,W\}$; $\lambda = \frac{1}{|E(i)+E(j)|}$, $\alpha^\tau, \beta^\tau \geq 0$ and $\frac{\alpha^\tau}{\beta^\tau} \geq E(\cdot)$, so that the trajectory $x_k(t) = \left\{(x_k^i(t), x_k^j(t)),\ t_0 \leq t\right\}$ is bounded in the unit square $\mathrm{C} = [0,1]\times[0,1]$.

We simply introduce the specific behavioral rule (6.7), the substitution of expected payoffs (6.1), and after some algebraic manipulation, we can obtain the **worker's replicator dynamic (RD)** system and the **firm's replicator dynamic (RD)** system driven by imitation:

$$\dot{x}_S = -\dot{x}_{NS} = x_S\left(1 - x_S\right)A. \tag{6.9}$$

$$\dot{y}_I = -\dot{y}_{NI} = y_I\left(1 - y_I\right)B. \tag{6.10}$$

Where A and B are defined by,

$$A = \alpha^W\left[\frac{y_I\left(\overline{p} - p\right) + s - \overline{s} + CE}{y_I\left(p + \overline{p}\right) + s + \overline{s} - CE}\right],$$

$$B = \alpha^F\left[\frac{B_I(NS) - B_{NI}(NS) + x_S\left(\Delta B_I + \Delta B_{NI} - \Delta P\right) - p}{B_I(NS) + B_{NI}(NS) + x_S\left(\Delta B_I - \Delta B_{NI} - \Delta P - 2s - 2\overline{s}\right) - p + 2s}\right],$$

where: $\Delta B_I = B_I(S) - B_I(NS)$, $\Delta B_{NI} = B_{NI}(NS) - B_{NI}(S)$ and $\Delta P = \overline{p} - p$.

6.1.2 Stability and Equilibria Analysis

The RD system, $(\dot{y}_I, \dot{x}_S)$, admits five stationary states or dynamic equilibria, i.e., $(0,0)$, $(0,1)$, $(1,0)$, $(1,1)$ and $(\hat{y}_I, \hat{x}_S)$, where:

$$\hat{y}_I = \frac{CE-(\bar{s}-s)}{\bar{p}-p},$$
$$\hat{x}_S = \frac{B_I(NS)-B_{NI}(NS)-p-CI}{B_I(NS)-B_I(S)+B_{NI}(S)-B_{NI}(NS)+(\bar{p}-p)}. \quad (6.11)$$

In fact, an interesting case occurs when $G=(\hat{y}_I,\hat{x}_S)$ is an equilibrium lying in the interior of the square $\mathbf{C}=[0,1]\times[0,1]$, which occurs when $0<\hat{y}_I<1$ and $0<\hat{x}_S<1$. The next proposition summarizes the evolutionary dynamics for the replicator dynamics of firms and workers:

Theorem. *The evolutionary dynamics* $(\dot{y}_I,\dot{x}_S)$ *of firms and workers driven by imitation are as follows:*

i. Equilibria $(1,0)$ *and* $(0,1)$ *are nodal sources and unstable.*

ii. Equilibria $(0,0)$ *and* $(1,1)$ *are asymptotically stable points or nodal sinks, and therefore ESSs against the field.*

iii. Equilibrium $G=(\hat{y}_I,\hat{x}_S)$ *is a saddle point, and therefore a threshold since it separates the basins of attraction of the low-level and high-level equilibria.*

A graphic representation is given in the following Figure 6-1:

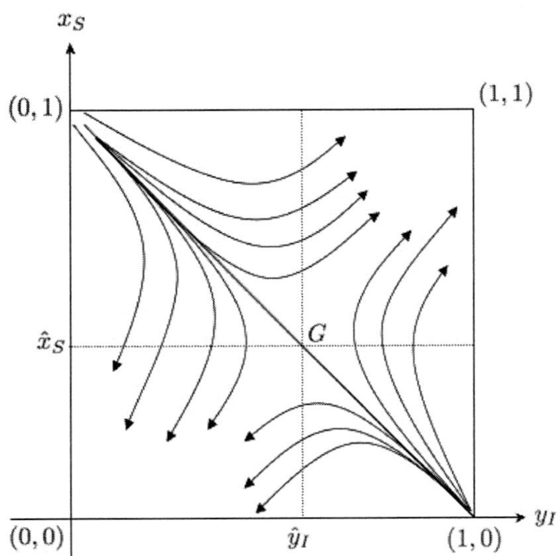

Figure 6-1. Vector field of the replicator system $(\dot{y}_I,\dot{x}_S)$.

Point G is hypothetically centered but this is not necessarily always the case since it depends on the parameters. These equilibria can be interpreted as follows:

i. Equilibrium $(0,0)$ is the low-level equilibrium in which firms and workers decide a low-profile $\{NI, NS\}$.

ii. Equilibrium $(0,1)$ and $(1,0)$ is a mismatch of profiles $\{NI, S\}$, $\{I, NS\}$.

iii. Equilibrium $(1,1)$ is the high-level equilibrium in which firms and workers decide a high-profile $\{I, S\}$.

Therefore, it is the rational behavior of the economic agents, firms and workers acting under imitation which can lead the economy into a poverty trap, and for which a threshold to overcome it exists.

Let us consider the case in which education costs may help us to overcome a poverty trap.

6.1.3 How to Overcome a Poverty Trap: Going for Education Costs

Since the results of the model depend on initial conditions – that is, the profile distributions, y_F and x_W –, we say that the model is historically dependent where an optimal strategy of the dynamic replicator system converges towards two distinct attractors, $(0,0)$ and $(1,1)$.

Let us denote by $y^F = (y_I^F, y_{NI}^F)$ and $x^W = (x_S^W, x_{NS}^W)$ the initial distributions of firms and workers. Consequently, the following case may arise.

This consideration can be analyzed as a game against the field in which there is no specific opponent to a given agent, payoffs depend on what everyone in the population is doing, and you are facing the other population state. That is, from the side of workers, an individual worker is playing against the field represented by the profile distribution of firms and workers (this is the population state).

Hence, let us consider the population of workers. If the fraction of innovative firms, y_I^F, is smaller than the threshold value $\hat{y}_I^F$, i.e.,

$$y_I^F < \hat{y}_I^F = \frac{CE - (\bar{s} - s)}{\bar{p} - p}, \tag{6.12}$$

then all potential workers prefer not to become high-skilled, and thus the initial distribution of workers $x^W(t_0)=(x_S^W(t_0),x_{NS}^W(t_0))\rightarrow(0,1)$ in pure strategies. Suppose, now, that a small portion of the non-innovative firms become innovative, $y'^F=\left(y'^F_I, y'^F_{NI}\right)$ where $y(t_0)<y'^F_I<y_I^F$, then workers prefer to be unskilled and the population of the high-skilled workers continues to decrease. In this case, a worker will be unskilled. So, we need a big change in the distribution of the population of firms to obtain for workers to become skilled. The threshold value is $\hat{y}_I^F$, if the new distribution verifies that $y_I^F>\hat{y}_I^F$, and therefore the rational imitator worker chooses to be skilled.

Now, we define an ESS against the field as follows:

Definition 23. *Consider a two population normal form game where each population, F and W, has two possible behaviors, 1 and 2. Suppose that the distribution of the population F is given by* $y_F=(y_{1F},y_{2F})$. *We say that the strategy* $x_W^*=(x_{1W}^*,x_{2W}^*)$ *is an ESS against the field if there exists an* ε *such that if*

$$E^W(x_W^*,y_F^{'})\geq E^W(x_W,y_F^{'}) \tag{6.13}$$

for all $x_W\in S_W$ *where* $|\,y_F-y_F^{'}\,|\leq\varepsilon$. *Therefore, if the distribution of the initial population of firms is given by* $y^F=(y_I^F,y_{NI}^F)$ *where* $y_I^F<\hat{y}_I^F$, *then* $x^W=(0,1)$ *is an ESS against the field.*

To overcome a poverty trap requires that we change the rationally determined outcome. To do so requires that the economy move beyond the threshold point of low-skilled workers and non-innovative firms. Focusing on workers, a central planner could implement a policy that decreases the costs of becoming high-skilled, or, given the incentive to become an innovative firm, to increase rewards to skilled workers.

Therefore, to reverse the inequality (6.12), and to overcome the poverty trap, consider the following.

i. Either costs of education *CE* must decrease or the differences in skill premia $\Delta P=\overline{p}-p$ must increase positively. Consequently, with a perturbation σ_ε, workers will become skilled and firms will become innovative and both perform better. The economy simultaneously overcomes its historic poverty trap. We thus consider the perturbation as a shock that compels agents to adopt new strategies, i.e., alternative strategies will invade the equilibrium as a consequence of the exogenous shock and, because the economy is in the basin of attraction of the higher-level equilibrium, the economy will converge to the higher-level equilibrium.

ii. Decreasing CE means investing in human capital, which implies an increasing ΔP. In particular, from equation (6.11), the threshold $\hat{x}_S = 0$ if given the gross benefits of firms (determined in the market), $B_i(j)$, $\forall\ i \in \{I, NI\}$, $j \in \{S, NS\}$, then the premia of unskilled workers is equal to $p = B_{NI}(NS) - B_I(S) - CI$, which means that an innovative firm must offer a premium which encourages the unskilled workers to supply their labor or become employed in the R&D sector. In turn, due to imitation and to strategic complementarities, such an unskilled worker must become a skilled worker. This means that workers with better profiles should get the largest possible premium, $\bar{p}$. In this way, the number of innovative firms (R&D) and the number of skilled workers (human capital) are large enough to overcome the poverty trap, i.e.

$$\left(x_S^W, y_I^F\right) > \left(\hat{x}_S^W, \hat{y}_I^F\right).$$

Any situation in the game against the field can be modified by a government or policy-maker that is capable, through economic policy, of changing the profile distributions y_F and x_W. Therefore, the appropriate economic policies that encourage education of the population, firms' investment in R&D and the strengthening of institutions in general, will help to overcome a poverty trap.

Alternatively, each player who wonders whether their current behavior is the optimal response for the long-run outcome of the economy could hypothetically participate in collective action to change their profiles. Either way, the economy becomes more efficient. The market alone is incapable of overcoming this kind of poverty trap. Policy-makers could intervene, for instance, by providing some kind of financial incentive for R&D investment or by imposing a minimum period of schooling.

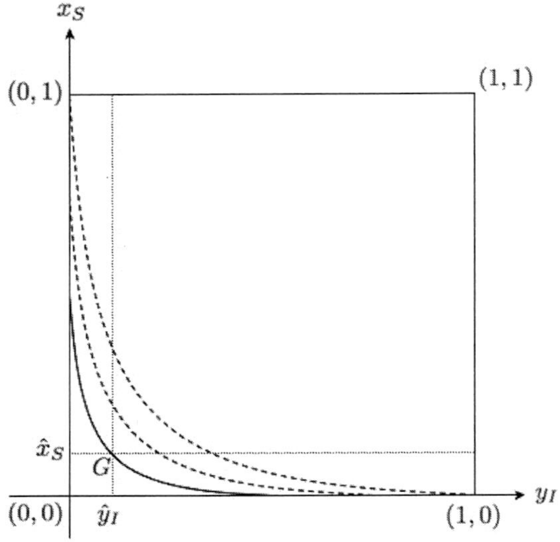

Figure 6-2. Decreasing the G-value through education costs, skill premia and payoff taxation.

In particular, education costs should be equal to the net difference (after taxes) in salaries from the high and low-skilled worker. If such a policy intervention occurs, then the basin of attraction for the high-level equilibrium expands (and the basin of attraction of the low-level equilibrium contracts, see Figure 6-2).

6.2 Replicator Dynamics with Fiscal Incentives

Focusing on firms, the central planner could implement a policy that would increase the number of innovative firms above the threshold. One policy option is to give fiscal incentives to those firms that implement skill premia, which can be provided for by a well-implemented income tax.

Let us assume that the policy-maker imposes some income tax at rate $\gamma \in [0,1]$ and $\delta \in [0,1]$ for firms and workers, respectively. $(\gamma = 0, \delta = 0)$ means *non-intervention* and $(\gamma = 1, \delta = 1)$ means *complete intervention.*

Suppose that when this policy starts, the economy has the following characteristics:

- Let N_i^τ be the total of i-strategists, $i \in \{(I, NI);(S, NS)\}$, from the population $\tau \in \{F, W\}$, and let $H = \sum_{i,\tau} N_i^\tau$ be the total number of players of the whole economy, normalized to 1.

- The mass (or number) of firms and workers that adopt a strategy i, $\forall i \in \{(I, NI);(S, NS)\}$, is given by:
-

$$m_i = \frac{N_i^\tau}{H} \quad (6.14) \text{ or:}$$

$$m_I = \frac{N_I^F}{H},\ m_{NI} = \frac{N_{NI}^F}{H},\ m_S = \frac{N_S^W}{H},\ m_{NS} = \frac{N_{NS}^W}{H}. \quad (6.15)$$

Then, we denote by $\Delta = \{m \in R_+^k \ : \ \sum_{i=1}^k m_i = 1\}$ the simplex of R_k. In our case, $k = 4$. If such taxes are imposed on each population $\tau \in \{F, W\}$, then the total revenue collected in the economy is:

$$T = \gamma[m_I E(I) + m_{NI} E(NI)] + \delta[m_S E(S) + m_{NS} E(NS)] \quad (6.16)$$

The implemented policy is characterized by taxation and subsidies. The subsidies are awarded to skilled workers and innovative firms. A proportion $\theta \in (0,1)$ of the total tax revenue collected is shared with skilled workers and the rest with innovative firms.

The new expected payoff, after transfers, for strategist S and NS are now respectively:

$$\begin{aligned} E_T(S) &= E(S)(1-\delta) + \theta T \\ E_T(NS) &= E(NS)(1-\delta). \end{aligned} \quad (6.17)$$

And for strategist I and NI, the new expected payoffs are now respectively:

$$\begin{aligned} E_T(I) &= E(I)(1-\gamma) + (1-\theta)T \\ E_T(NI) &= E(NI)(1-\gamma). \end{aligned} \quad (6.18)$$

So the dynamical system (6.8), $\forall \ i, j \in \{(I, NI);(S, NS)\}$, is now substituted by the new dynamical system given by:

$$\dot{x}_i^\tau = x_i^\tau (1 - x_i^\tau) [\lambda(\alpha^\tau + \boldsymbol{\beta}^\tau)(E_T(i) - E_T(j))]. \quad (6.19)$$

Consider that the initial conditions are $z(t_0) = (x_S(t_0), y_I(t_0))$, then the solution to this system will be unique and symbolized by $\xi(t, t_0 z(t_0))$. The threshold value corresponding to this system is given by the equations:

$$\begin{aligned} E_T(S) &= E(NS) - \tfrac{\theta T}{1-\delta} \\ E_T(I) &= E(NI) - \tfrac{(1-\theta)T}{(1-\gamma)} \end{aligned} \qquad (6.20)$$

From these equations, we obtain the threshold value in terms of the share of skilled workers and innovative firms, and these values are given by:

$$\begin{aligned} n_S &= \hat{x}_S - \tfrac{(1-\theta)T}{1-\delta} \tfrac{1}{B_I(NS) - B_I(S) + B_{NI}(S) - B_{NI}(NS) - p + \bar{p}}, \\ n_I &= \hat{y}_I - \tfrac{\theta T}{1-\gamma} \tfrac{1}{\bar{p} - p}. \end{aligned} \qquad (6.21)$$

Where $\hat{y}_I$ and $\hat{x}_S$ are the former threshold value defined in (6.11).

So, if the initial value $z(t_0) = (x_S(t_0), y_I(t_0))$ in a time $t = t_0$ of the economy is below the threshold value $G = (\hat{x}_S, \hat{y}_I)$, then the policy-maker needs to implement taxes such that:

$$\begin{aligned} x_S(t_0) &\geq \hat{x}_S - \tfrac{(1-\theta)T}{1-\delta} \tfrac{1}{B_I(NS) - B_I(S) + B_{NI}(S) - B_{NI}(NS) - p + \bar{p}}, \\ y_I(t_0) &\geq \hat{y}_I - \tfrac{\theta T}{1-\gamma} \tfrac{1}{\bar{p} - p}, \end{aligned} \qquad (6.22)$$

and therefore the initial conditions are outside of the basin of attraction of the low-level equilibrium, corresponding to equations system (6.19). So, the economy moves toward a high-level equilibrium. When the economy passes the threshold value G, the policy-makers may leave the economy to evolve by its own rules, i.e., the evolution of the economy will be determined by system (6.8), but now the initial conditions are in the basin of attraction of the high-level equilibrium. This means that the policy-makers should withdraw taxation and subsidies once the economy, following a trajectory corresponding to a solution of (6.19), surpasses G. Subsequently, the agents, following their imitation rule, will drive the economy to a high-level equilibrium. Therefore, the intervention of the policy-makers in the economy at time $t = t_0$, could be justified for a given time period of $z(t_0)$ below the threshold value G.

Summarizing, the policy-makers could intervene in the economy by implementing a *tax and subsidy policy*, such that it encourages workers to become skilled and firms to become innovative. The purpose of this policy is to withdraw the economy from a trajectory converging to an inefficient equilibrium (a poverty trap). This intervention by the policy-maker ends once the solution of the dynamical system given by (6.19) $\xi(t,t_0,z(t_0))$ surpasses the threshold value G, because from this moment, the economy will follow a trajectory corresponding to a solution of the dynamical system (6.8), of high growth, converging to a high level equilibrium. The participation of the social planner in the economy from then on would be superfluous.

6.3 Concluding Remarks

The model we presented here is practical and implementable, for instance the Bombardier Aeronautica Firm in Queretaro (Mexico) is a real approximation of our model. A recent article in the *Latin Trade Magazine*, 'Mexico's Jet Set'[31], parallels our research. The article discusses the role of innovative firms, human capital requirements, imitation, skill premia, and decreasing the costs of education in the aeronautical industry. Given the conditions, the recommendations follow from our model.

From our model, a policy-maker may implement an incentive-based policy to reach the high-level equilibrium of innovative firms and skilled workers; for instance, to implement a policy to lower the cost of education. Also, policy-makers can provide a tax scheme that encourages R&D investment, or they can impose a minimum level of high-quality education for the whole population. However, the policy-makers' intervention in the economy can end once the economy passes the threshold value.

Conversely, a poverty trap arises because agents imitate the best-responding strategies when the state of the economy lacks both R&D and human capital. For low numbers of skilled labor, innovation will not be profitable, not just in terms of final output but also in terms of the generated rate of technical change. Only after an economy is sufficiently developed in terms of its supply and demand for skilled labor will deliberate R&D be undertaken. So, in this case, one of the main obstacles to overcoming a poverty trap is the agents' imitative behavior.

---

[31] Available at http://latintrade.com/2009/12/mexico%E2%80%99s-jet-set and accessed 8 February 2010.

Using evolutionary game theory to tackle the problem of poverty traps, we conclude that a kind of bounded rationality characterized by imitation offers a hint to understanding the dynamics of poverty traps. Boundedly rational agents act to maximize their own payoffs, pursuing their own self-interest as best as they can. Hence, we have shown the strategic foundations of high and low level equilibria when firms and workers imitate and thus they adopt the best strategy given the state of the economy.

Future research could offer a feasible answer about the magnitudes of government intervention, and the lengths of time required to enact change, specifically, how large should governments' subsidies of R&D be, and for how long should government subsidize R&D activities and human capital accumulation? Solving these questions could improve policy prescriptions in the context of economies where we believe imitation, or a version thereof, is the behavioral rule that firms and workers are most likely to follow.

CHAPTER SEVEN

ECONOMIC AGENTS AND DEVELOPMENT

Stiglitz (1998) states that economic development represents a transformation of society driven by the behavior of economic agents and their relationships, ways of thinking, ways of addressing the problems of health and education, and production methods, and other modern forms [innovative]. Hence, by "economic development," we mean economic, social and political processes in a specific geographic area – within the boundaries of an economy (country or nation) dynamic – resulting in behavior, actions and interactions of agents (economic, political, and social) that reside in that geographic area, and aims to increase social welfare steadily and sustainably.

Therefore, we claim that economic agents may be of high profile or low profile. Economic agents must decide to be one of these characteristics. If an economic agent decides to be high profile, it means that this agent improves the social economic welfare because he/she is an agent/individual that is part of any of the following characteristics: i) human capital, ii) innovative firms, iii) efficient institutions, iv) democratic governments, v) honest or not corrupt. The situation is otherwise when an economic agent decides to be low-profile (non-innovative firms, corrupt behavior, unskilled workers, inefficient institution, and so on). Because we consider strategic complementarities, high profile agents prefer to interact with high profile agents, and low profiles prefer to do so with low profiles.

Stiglitz and Hoff (2001) show that the gap between rich and poor countries are due to important differences, such as the differences in economic organization, the "interaction of agents" (owners of the sources of growth factors) and institutions that mediate these interactions, and decisions made by such agents with respect to the characterized profile of production.

However, if the decisions of economic agents are not coordinated with each other, a problem of multiple equilibria may arise: either high-equilibria or poverty traps (see Bowles, 1995; Accinelli and Sanchez Carrera, 2012; Sanchez Carrera, 2012). Inertial self-reinforcement is a story of multiple equilibria, and therefore directs our attention to the beliefs or expectations of the economic agents which shore up one or another of the equilibria. In particular, one might ask how the formation of such expectations may be significantly conditioned by history. So impediments to economic development include coordination problems as a result of externalities and/or decisions of agents regarding their profile features that may arise in matters relating to:

- Activities Research and Development (R&D, Research and Development). Firms that perform R&D investments can have positive effects, not included in the market mechanism of other firms. On the other hand, increased R&D stock in a sector may lead to the increased profitability of individual companies in R&D investments. Conversely, low levels in the stock of R&D sectors can lead to a "balance of underdevelopment," which is caused by the low incentive for each company to invest in R&D (Krugman, 1995; Romer, 1986);
- The behavior of bureaucrats; Annuitants and Collective Performance. For example, a bureaucrat (or annuitant) has less incentive to innovate than an innovator. Traps balance can result when the ratio of bureaucrats dominates the population of an economy. The effects of a case of "collective enforcement" (when an agent punishes the set of agents) versus "individual execution" (when an agent to another agent punishes a group of agents) is analyzed by Greif (1994). With low levels of development, balance is dominated by the actions of collective execution. The balance with individual execution allows the emergence of formal executions delegated to the government;
- Distribution of Property. The distribution of this may affect the proportion of companies established in a society and the proportion of workers. On balance, low levels of development, i.e. the proportion of the population that undertakes business activities, is low because of the low level of wealth of the agents;
- The costs of finding skilled workers. Firms that adopt new technologies require workers with skills for consistent implementation thereof. With regard to generating new technologies and providing appropriate training for workers, when these two activities are are performed within the company, the results are profitable for the company. When these two activities are separated and the costs for firms and workers are high, then traps equilibrium with low skill levels of both the workforce and innovation can occur (Acemoglu, 1997).

In what follows, we show the role of the government, arguing that public policy should focus on building capacities that are beyond the ability of the market to provide, so as to incentivize economic agents to become high profile. This shifts the debate towards a neutral role of the government as a builder of capacities that enable economic agents to realize their potential (Salamon 2002). Hence, economic development occurs when individual agents have the opportunity to develop the capacities that allow them to actively engage and contribute to the economy, i.e. high-profile economic agents that strengthen economic development.

7.1. The model

Consider that economies, *E*, are composed of populations of economic agents. Assume that there are two-populations of economic agents, namely *A* and *B*. The population of economic agents *A* is composed of low-profile economic agents, A_l, and high-profile, A_h. The population of economic agents B is in turn composed of low-profile economic agents, B_l, and high-profile, B_h. So this economy can be defined by the following list:

$$E = \{\Omega = \{A_x, B_x\}; U = \{U_{Ax}, U_{Bx}\}; S(x,x)\}$$

where Ω is the set of types $x = \{h,l\}$ of economic agents from populations $\{A,B\}$. U is the set of utility functions for each $x-$type of economic agent from population $\{A,B\}$. The social utility function or social welfare is represented by $S(i,j)$ and this function will be described below.

Consider that in each period t, economic agents from one population, *A* or *B*, are matched with an economic agent from the other population, *A* or *B*. There are strategic complementarities. That is, the low-profile economic agents of population A prefer to be matched with low-profile economic agents of population B; similarly, the high-profile economic agents of population A prefer to be matched with high-profile economic agents of population B; and the same applies to those agents from population B matching agents from population A.

Assume that economic agents of population A are stratified according to their income levels. This will be explained below. In short, economic agents from population *A* may represent, for example, citizens, while economic agents of population, *B*, represent the rulers, public servants or even the institutions given in this economy. Hence, the economy *E* has the following characteristics:

1. We claim that an economic agent is high-profile if he/she meets or is responsible for aspects (like being a taxpayer, or being part of human capital, R&D activities, property rights, social justice, equal opportunity, efficient institutions, and so on) that mean that social welfare is potentiated. Otherwise, the economic agent is low profile. For instance, economic agents from population A are of high-profiles, h , if they meet their fiscal obligations, responsibilities and other aspects that help to achieve greater social welfare. Otherwise, we say that they are low-profile economic agents, l, from population A who do not meet these aspects and harm social welfare. We assume, then, that $A = A_h \bigcup A_l$, and also that $A_h \bigcap A_l = \phi$. The same is true for the case of population B. Population B, is in turn composed of high-profile B_h and low-profile B_l , verifying that $B = B_h \bigcup B_l$, and $B_h \bigcap B_l = \phi$.
2. The share of types, h and l , of economic agents from each population is time-variant. Hence, in every period of time t we represent by:
   $\alpha_A(t)$ the share/fraction of $A-$economic agents of high-profile;
   $\gamma_B(t)$ the share/fraction of $B-$ economic agents of high-profile;
   $\beta_A(t) = 1 - \alpha_A(t)$ the share/fraction of $A-$ economic agents of low-profile; and
   $\delta_B(t) = 1 - \gamma_B(t)$ the share/fraction of $B-$ economic agents of low profile.

In this vein, we state the following.

Definition 24. *Let the index $l(t)$ be a measure of the proportional amount of economic agents of low-profile that exist in the economy, i.e.* $l(t) = \beta_A(t) + \delta_B(t)$.

We consider that only economic agents from population A are distributed according to their levels of income, denoted by a set Y . All of them are likely to be taxpayers. Consider that the probability that an economic agent $x \in A$ has income lower or equal to $y \in Y$ is:

$$P(y(x) \leq y) = P(y).$$

Note that this probability corresponds to the fraction of economic agents with income lower than or equal to y. We assume that according to their income level, citizens are divided into n different groups, $I_1, I_2 ...., I_n$, thus $y : A \rightarrow I$ where $I = \{I_1, ... I_n\}$, so $y(x) \in I$. By $n(I_i)$ we denote the share of citizens in the level I_i.

By $y(x)$ we denote the income of the economic agent $x \in A$. They are likely taxpayers, so their net income is given by $\tau(y)y(x)$, where $0 < \tau(y) < 1$. That is, tax rates are proportional to income levels, i.e. $\tau(y) = \tau(I_i)$ for all $y \in I_i, i = 1,...., n$.

Notice that, any policy maker should fix the optimal tax rate assuming that all economic agents from A pay taxes. However, this is no longer optimal in the presence of low-profile economic agents. Suppose the share of high-profile economic agents that are taxpayers in time t is $\alpha(t) = \alpha$. Consider in addition that $P_\alpha(I_i)$ corresponds to the proportion of economic agents in the level I_i, $i = 1,..., n$ that in time t are paying taxes to be characterized as high-profile agents.

The lowest and highest levels of income are denoted by $\underline{y}$ and $\overline{y}$, respectively. Hence:

- $P_\alpha(y)$ denotes the probability that a citizen $x \in A$ with income y is paying an income tax corresponding to $\tau(y)y(x)$ when the total percentage of taxpayers are those economic agents of high-profile, which is given by α.
- Thus, income distribution $P_\alpha(y)$ is concentrated in the interval $[\underline{y}, \overline{y}]$. Total national revenues due to taxation in time t are:

$$T_t = \int_{\underline{y}}^{\overline{y}} \tau(y)y(x)dP_\alpha(y) = \sum_{i=1}^{n} \tau(I_i)y(I_i)\Delta P_\alpha(I_i). \qquad (7.1)$$

We consider that the matching between types of economic agents, each belonging to one of the two populations, is given in each period of time. If being an economig agent of low-profile is punished, the total amount received by the payment of fines is transferred to improve social welfare. So the total money obtained by the central authority is the sum of the total amount of taxes collected plus the total amount received from fines. However, the total amount of fines is a random variable, W, but with an expected value $\overline{W}$. So, the government or policy maker has an expected total national revenue:

$R_t = T_t + \overline{W}_t > 0.$ (7.2)

Individuals A and B must have some utility due to the tax system and national revenue. That is, utilities of economic agents from A and from B, $u_A(\alpha, R_t) > 0$ and $u_B(\alpha, R_t) > 0$, depend on the total national revenue, R_t, and on the share, α, of high-profile economic agents which are taxpayers.

Consider the next definition.

Definition 25. *The level of economic development increases with the total national revenue and with the share of high-profile economic agents, i.e.*

$$\frac{\partial u_\Omega}{\partial R}(\alpha, R_t) > 0 \quad \text{and} \quad \frac{\partial u_\Omega}{\partial \alpha}(\alpha, R_t) > 0,$$

$$\text{for all } \Omega = \{A_x, B_x\}, x \in \{l, h\},$$

and functions $u_\Omega(\alpha, R_t)$ *are concave with respect to* R_t, *i.e.* $\frac{\partial^2 u_\Omega(\alpha, R_t)}{\partial R_t^2} < 0$, *where economic agents from* A *and from* B *do not equally value the welfare obtained by taxes, but this is considered in the fact that* $u_{Ax}(\alpha, R_t)$ *is not necessarily equal to* $u_{Bx}(\alpha, R_t)$.

Therefore, under the above considerations, we can state that the expected amount of tax collected can be written as:

$$T_\alpha(t) = \sum_0^{n-1} \tau(I_i)[y(I_{i+1}) - y(I_i)P_\alpha(I_{i+1}, t)],$$

where, as we said, $P_\alpha(I_{i+1}, t)$ represents the percentage/share of economic agents from A with income $y(I_{i+1})$ that are of high-profile by being taxpayers, in time *t*. Whereas that total (potential) amount collected corresponds to:

$$T_{\alpha=1} = \sum_0^{n-1} \tau(I_{i+1})[y(I_{i+1}) - y(I_i)P_{\alpha=1}(I_{i+1})]$$

where $P_{\alpha=1}(I_{i+1})$ is the share of high-profile economic agents which are taxpayers with income $y_{I_{i+1}}$, while $P(I_{i+1})$ is the total share of individuals with such an income in the population *A*. So $P(I_i) \geq P_\alpha(I_i, t)$ for all *t*, with equality if and only if $\alpha = 1$; that is the case when all economic agents are of high-profile.

From now, to facilitate writing, if not being strictly necessary, we will suppress the variable t, although all values depend on the distribution of populations, which certainly change over time. Here, we are interested in finding an optimal tax rate for economic agents with the scope of improving the social welfare in the economy. We assume that the government or policy maker is benevolent and wants to work towards greater social welfare. For this calculation, assume that τ represents the policy tax.

Hence, the utility of an economic agent x from subpopulation A can be written as:

$$u_{A_x}(\alpha,\tau) = u_x\left(\alpha, \sum_0^{n-1} \tau(y(I_{i+1})[y(I_{i+1}) - y(I_i)]P_\alpha(I_{i+1}) + \overline{W}\right) + \\ + (1-\tau(I_j))y(I_j).$$

To simplify the notation, we denote by τ_j the optimal tax corresponding to the economic agent with a level of income equal to y_{I_j}, $j = 1,2...,n$, i.e. $\tau_j = \tau(I_j)$. The following statement provides an important result.

> Theorem 7. *As long as the income inequality between two neighboring social classes (measured by different income I_I) increases, tax evasion increases (i.e. more are low-profile economic agents), and so the levels of development in this economy are lower.*

Proof. Any central authority or government may assume that every citizen must pay taxes according with their income, i.e: $\alpha = 1$, then the utility function depends only on taxes τ, and so the optimal tax rate $\tau^*(y)$ (the optimal policy for the central planner) must verify the equation:

$$\frac{\partial u_{A_x}}{\partial \tau_j}(\tau_j^*) = \frac{\partial u_A}{\partial I}\left(1, \Sigma_0^{n-1} \tau_{i+1}^*[y(I_{i+1}) - y(I_i)]P_{\alpha=1}(I_{i+1})\right) \\ [y(I_j) - y(I_{j-1})]P_{\alpha=1}(I_j) - y(I_j) = 0 \tag{7.3}$$

or equivalently,

$$\frac{\partial u_A}{\partial R}\left(1, \sum_0^{n-1} \tau_{i+1}^*[y(I_{i+1}) - y(I_i)]P_{\alpha=1}(I_{i+1})\right)\frac{\Delta y(I_j)}{y(I_j)} P_{\alpha=1}(I_j) = 1, \tag{7.4}$$

where $\Delta y(I_j) = y(x_j) - y(I_{j-1})$ is the income gap between the social classes I_j and I_{j-1}. Note that if we assume $\alpha = 1$, then $P_{\alpha=1}(x_j)$ is equal to the total percentage of citizens with income $x \leq I_j$. Given that the utility function is strictly concave in R, it follows that $\frac{\partial^2 u_{A_x}}{\partial \tau_j^2} < 0$ so, τ_j^* is a maximun. In conclusion, from equation (7.4) and Definition 25, we get that the number of economic agents that are willing to be high-profile is a decreasing function of the gap between social classes I_j and I_{j-1}, and that is income inequality. Hence, as the gap between social classes becomes lower, and/or the lower the income inequality, the higher the levels of economic development.

However, there may be economic agents of population B wishing to be low-profile, and by the strategic complementarities, those economic agents are looking to be matched with low-profile agents too. This is analyzed in the next section.

7.2. On the Evolutionary Dynamics

In this section, we model the evolution of the behavior of the types of economic agents in both populations A and B. This is done by techniques from evolutionary game theory. We consider an asymmetrical set of two different populations whose individuals choose strategically between two behaviors or pure strategies, l and h, low-profile and high-profile. To analyze the evolution of the behavior of economic agents, we accept that the policy of income tax determined by the government is optimal, then a dynamic system modeling imitative behavior and mutual interaction between those economic agents results in a dynamic type system – Volterra Lotka (1956) – in which the parameters are strongly related to the degree of economic development and a good control system.

The choice of the future strategy (low-profile or high-profile) by economic agents, is performed under conditions of imperfect information, either because agents do not know the exact probability distributions needed to assess the expected values associated with some possible behavior or because they are not capable of performing calculations in the finite time that this operation involves. In this framework, we assume that:

1. All economic agents seek to maximize their welfare under uncertainty without exact knowledge of the chances of success associated with each of the possible behaviors.
2. Under these circumstances, they choose to imitate the behavior of

their more successful neighbors or the behavior of those who they consider leaders. Observing the behavior of those agents, they may intuit the chances of success associated with possible strategies. This is captured by the parameters b and f in the following dynamical system (ref equation: dincrr; see below). According to their beliefs, they will choose the behavior which is more profitable, given the current state of the economy. Therefore, these beliefs are strongly related to the perception of agents about government efficiency in facing low-profile economic agents.

3. It is also natural to assume that the behavior of each agent from each population is influenced by the behavior of the counterparty. For example, it is natural to assume that the growth rate of the low-profile agents of population B, given by $\frac{\dot{\delta}}{\delta}$, decreases as the relative weight of the high-profile agents of population A increases. Recall that $\beta = 1 - \alpha$ and $\gamma = 1 - \delta$, and that all these variables must be non-negative at each point in time t.
4. Note that if at some point t_f, $\alpha(t_f) = 1$, then for every $t > t_f$ implies that $\dot{\delta}(t) < 0$ and $\dot{\alpha}(t) = 0$. Conversely, if in a given time, any agent in population B is low-profile, then each agent in population A is a low-profile, then $\dot{\alpha}(t) < 0$ and $\dot{\delta}(t) = 0$.

Definition 26. *For the evolution of the percentage or fraction of low-profile (and high-profile) economic agents in time $t = t_0$, assuming that $t = t_0$, $0 < \alpha(t_0) < 1$ and $0 < \delta(t_0) < 1$, we use the following system of differential equations:*

$$\begin{aligned} \dot{\alpha} &= \alpha(a + b\alpha - c\delta), \\ \dot{\beta} &= -\dot{\alpha}, \\ \dot{\delta} &= \delta(d - e\alpha + f\delta), \\ \dot{\gamma} &= -\dot{\delta}. \end{aligned} \tag{7.5}$$

where a, b, c, d, e, f are positive constants, and that magnitudes of these parameters are directly related to the policy pursued by the government, particularly the fines and the probability that pervailing low-profile *behaviors can be caught and punished. For example, the c parameter in the first equation is reduced if m and $p(m)$ increase. Note that $-c\delta$ is the negative effect that an increased number of low-profile agents in population B has on the behavior of the high-profile agents of population A. The parameter b represents the importance of imitation within the subpopulation of high-profile economic agents from A ; this value increases with the difference: $u_{A_h}(\alpha, I, t) - u_{A_l}(\alpha, I)$.*

We assume that all economic agents of both populations A and B can change their behavior if a different behavior that can be imitated exists within its population. This leads us to conclude that if in time $t = t_f$, e.g. $\alpha(t_f) = 1$ then $\alpha(t) = 1$ for every $t \geq t_f$. This is similar to other cases, i.e. if $\beta(t_f) = 1$ then $\beta(t) = 1$ for every $t \geq t_f$ and is the same for the agents from *B*. So the dynamic system (7.5) can be reformulated as:

$$\dot{\alpha} = \begin{cases} \alpha(a + b\alpha - c\delta), & if \;\; 0 < \alpha(t_0) < 1, \\ \\ 0 & \forall\, t \geq t_f \; : \; \alpha(t_f) = 1, \;\; \alpha(t_f) = 0. \end{cases}$$

$$\dot{\delta} = \begin{cases} \\ \delta(d - e\alpha + f\delta), & 0 \\ \\ 0 & \forall\, t \geq t_f \; : \; \delta(t_f) = 1, \;\; \delta(t_f) = 0. \end{cases} \tag{7.6}$$

Notice that:

- Parameter *b* measures the effect of imitating behavior for the agents in population *A*. The growth rate of the behavior of high-profiles is greater as the influence of imitation in social behavior becomes greater, measured by b , i.e. $\frac{\partial(\frac{\dot{\alpha}}{\alpha})}{\partial \alpha} = b > 0$.
- The intensity of these parameters strongly depends on the difference between the utilities of the high-profile and low-profile agents. This shows that it is possible for the government to design a policy to ensure high-profile economic agents in both populations (see below equation 7.7).
- The pernicious effect on society of the low-profile behavioral agents in population B is strongly related to parameter c . Note that

$$\frac{\partial(\frac{\dot{\alpha}}{\alpha})}{\partial\delta} = -c < 0.$$

- Parameter e measures the rate at which low-profile agents in B decreases (by the effect of increased high-profile agents in A), and parameter f measures the speed at which the low-profiles in B increases (by the effect of an increase of the low-profile agents in B). This parameter is closely related to the role of imitation in society. That is:

$$\frac{\partial(\frac{\dot{\delta}}{\delta})}{\partial\alpha} = -e < 0, \quad \frac{\partial(\frac{\dot{\delta}}{\delta})}{\partial\delta} = f > 0. \tag{7.7}$$

By strategic complementarities, note that by choosing a low-profile behavior, the incentives of agents in B decrease with the increasing percentage of agents in A following a high-profile behavior. Therefore:

1. If $\delta > \frac{a+b}{\alpha}$ then $\dot{\alpha} < 0$, the growth rate of high-profile agents in A is negative. Thus, only in the case where δ is large enough, then you may see an increase in low-profile agents in A. This means that in the absence of low-profile agents in B, low-profile agents in A tends to disappear.
2. If we get that in a given period of time, $t = t_0$, the number of high-profiles in A is large enough, $\alpha(t_0) > \frac{c\delta-a}{b}$, then economic agents prefer to become high-profile. In the case where $\alpha(t_0) > \frac{c-a}{b}$, this preference does not depend on the number of low-profile agents in B. This possibility is given in the case where $\delta = 1$.

This shows once again that the main features of the system of differential equations are closely related to economic policies chosen by the government, and the efficiency of the institutional system in attacking the low-profiles and encourage the growth of high-profiles. The system (7.6) represents the structural dynamics of the behavior of low-profiles in B and high-profiles in A. According to this evolutionary system, the rate of low-profiles in this economy (see Definition 24) evolves according to the differential equation:

$$\dot{t}_c(t) = (1-\dot{\alpha}) + \dot{\delta}.$$

Note that it is not possible to obtain the analytical expression of the population status in a phase diagram, since:

$$\frac{d\alpha}{d\gamma}=\frac{\dot{\alpha}}{\dot{\gamma}}=\frac{\alpha(a+b\alpha-c\delta)}{\delta(d-e\alpha+f\delta)}$$

is not separable. However, we find expressions for the nullclinas or isoclines with zero slope, i.e. for curves in the phase space where $\dot{\alpha}=0$ or $\dot{\delta}=0$,

$$\begin{aligned} \mu &: \quad a+b\alpha-c\delta=0, \\ \nu &: \quad d-e\alpha+f\delta=0. \end{aligned} \tag{7.8}$$

Furthermore, it is noted that the region $[0,1]\times[=,1]$ is invarante for the dynamic system in (7.6). These considerations allow us to characterize dynamical system solutions somehow, depending on the initial conditions of the economy.

Theorem. *The dynamic system defined by (7.6) shows that economic agents of high-profile and low-profile coexist and evolve over time in both populations A and B. The relative percentage of each subpopulation or group depends on the economic policy ruled by the government and defined by the parameters of the dynamic system.*

Proof. Let us begin by noting that the region $[0,1]\times[0,1]$ is invariant for this system of differential equations (7.5 or 7.6), which means that the system solution will remain permanently in this region. Next, consider the nullclines phase diagram (represented by Figures 7-1 and 7-2 (ab)), then one of the different situations is true:

- The nullclineas intersect at $[0,1]\times[0,1]$, see Figure 7-7, and this is the case if $\frac{e}{f}<1$ and $\frac{b}{c}<\frac{e}{f}$.
- The nullclineas do not intersect at $[0,1]\times[0,1]$ (these cases are represented in Figures 7-8a and 7-8b), then
    - μ is below ν, and this is the case if $\frac{a}{c}<1$ and $\frac{b}{c}<\frac{e}{f}$, or alternatively,
    - $\frac{a}{c}>1$ and $\frac{e}{f}<1$, and also,
    - $\frac{a}{c}<1$ and $\frac{e}{f}>1$.

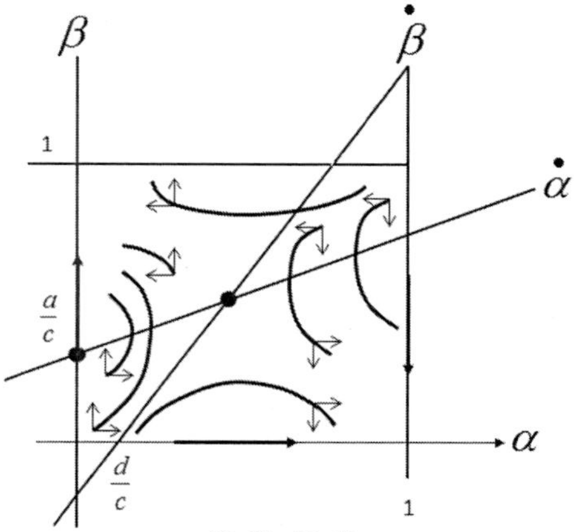

Figure 7-1. nullclineas intersect at $[0,1]\times[0,1]$.

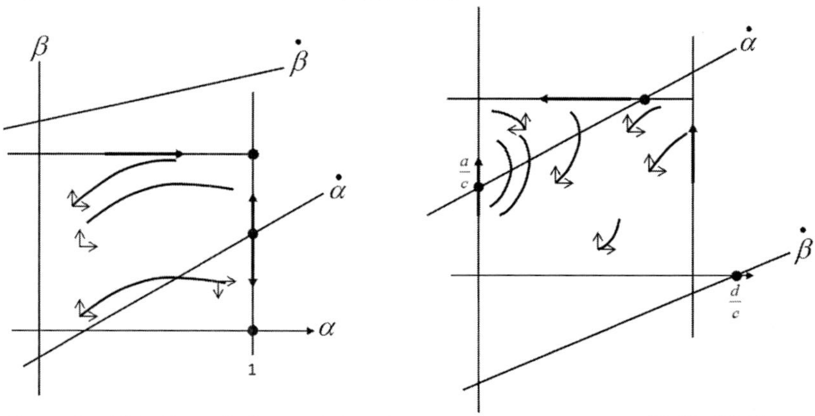

Figure 7-2(ab). The nullclines a-left and b-right do not intersect at $[0,1]\times[0,1]$.

The most relevant case is represented by the Figure 7-2a. Note that in this case, the initial relationship between the percentages of high-profile agents in A and low-profiles in B is the key to understanding the future evolution of the population. So, if the initial values verify:

$$0<\alpha(t_0)<-\frac{f\delta(t_0)+d}{e} \quad and \quad 1>\delta(t_0)>\frac{a+b\alpha(t_0)}{c},$$

then the population evolves so that all economic agents in A dislike being high-profile and every agent in B is low-profiles, i.e. an economy with low profiles economic agents. But if the initial number of high-profile economic agents in A is sufficiently large,

$$\alpha(t_0) > -\frac{f\delta(t_0)+d}{e} \quad and \quad \delta(t_0) < \frac{a+b\alpha(t_0)}{c},$$

the economy evolves to an idyllic world without low-profile economic agents. However, more realistic are the situations in which:

$$0 < \alpha(t_0) < -\frac{f\delta(t_0)+d}{e}, \quad and \quad 0 < \delta(t_0) < \frac{a+b\alpha(t_0)}{c},$$

or,

$$\alpha(t_0) > -\frac{f\delta(t_0)+d}{e} \quad and \quad \delta(t_0) > \frac{a+b\alpha(t_0)}{c},$$

because in these cases, the economy evolves to a steady state in which there are both a positive percentage of economic agents with high profiles and agents with low profiles in both populations A and B .

The final distribution of types of economic agents in the economy depends largely on the government intervention to develop institutional policies. That is, in terms of our model, the choice of economic policy means to implement the appropriate values for the parameters that encourage economic agents to have an imitative behavior and choose the high-profile type, so as to increase the level of economic development.

7.3 Concluding Remarks

We have developd a model to demonstrate that economic inequality of economic agents harms economic development. We have shown how the population of economic agents evolves into high or low profiles. Then, we have demonstrated that government intervention is crucial in order to encourage agents to decide to be high profile, and so to achieve economic development.

The model parameters, which are determined by the economic policies of the government, should be addressed to encourage economic agents to choose to be a high profile. For instance, employers reward professional success and innovativeness with higher wages or more prestigious jobs, which then translates into higher income. But underlying this ideal is the reality that agents are high profile, i.e. educated and prepared for gainful employment, and that high quality jobs are available, with opportunities for advancement. Reaching this objective requires government intervention, such that it encourages economic agents to be of high profile, since economic development requires effective institutions grounded in norms of openness, tolerance to risk, appreciation for diversity, and confidence in the realization of mutual gain for both the public and private sectors, driven by the behavior of their economic agents.

BIBLIOGRAPHY

Acemoglu, D., "Training and innovation in an imperfect labor market," *Review of Economic Studies* 64 (1997): 445-64.

—. "Why Do New Technologies Complement Skills? Directed Technical Change and Wage Inequality," *Quarterly Journal of Economics* 113 (1998): 1055-1089.

—. "Changes in Unemployment and Wage Inequality: An Alternative Theory and Some Evidence," *American Economic Review* 89 (1999): 1259-1278.

—. "Technical Change, Inequality and the Labor Market," *Journal of Economic Literature* 40 (2002): 7-72.

—. "Patterns of Skill Premia," *Review of Economic Studies* 70 (2003): 199-230.

—. "The Crisis of 2008: Structural Lessons for and from Economics" MIT notes, 2009.

Accinelli and Sanchez Carrera, E., "The Evolutionary Game of Poverty Traps," *The Manchester School* 80 (2012): 381-400.

—. "Strategic complementarities between innovative firms and skilled workers: the poverty trap and the policymaker's intervention," *Structural Change and Economic Dynamics*, 22 (2011): 30-40.

Accinelli, E. Brida, G. and Sanchez Carrera, E., Imitative Behavior in a Two Population Model. In *Advances in Dynamic Games. Applications, and Numerical Methods for Differential and Stochastic Games.* Dedicated to the Memory of Arik A. Melikyan. Series: *Annals of the International Society of Dynamic Games*, Vol. 11. Breton, Michèle; Szajowski, Krzysztof (Eds.). Springer-Verlag, 2009.

Aghion, P., "On Institutions and Growth," in *Institutions, Development, and Economics Growth,* Ed. Theo S. Eicher and García-Peñalosa. Cambridge: The MIT Press, 2006.

Aghion P. and Howitt P., "On the Macroeconomic Consequences of Major Technological Change," in *General Purpose Technologies and Economic Growth*, Ed. E. Helpman. Cambridge: MIT Press, 1999.

Alos-Ferrer and S. Weidenholzer, "Imitation, Local Interactions and Efficiency," *Economics Letters* 93 (2006): 163–168.

Apesteguia, J., S. Huck and J. Oechssler, "Imitation-theory and experimental evidence," *Journal of Economic Theory* 136 (2007): 217-235.

Azariadis, C., "The Economics of Poverty Traps; Part One: Complete Markets," *Journal of Economic Growth* 1 (1996): 449-486.

Azariadis, C. and Drazen, A., "Threshold Externalities in Economic Development," *The Quarterly Journal of Economics* 105 (1990): 501-26.

Azariadis, C. and Starchuski, H. "Poverty Traps" in Aghion, P. and Durlauf, S. (eds.) *Handbook of Economic Growth*, Elsevier, 2005.

Balkenborg, D. and K. Schlag, "On the evolutionary selection of sets of Nash equilibria," *Journal of Economic Theory* 133 (2007): 295-315.

Barret C. and B. Swallow, "Fractal Poverty Traps," *World Development* 34 (2006), pp. 1-15.

Benhabib J., Spiegel, M., "The role of human capital in economic development: Evidence from aggregate cross-country data," *Journal of Monetary Economics* 34 (1994): 143-173.

Berman, E., Bound, J. and Griliches, Z., "Changes in the Demand for Skilled Labor Within U.S. Manufacturing Industries: Evidence from the Annual Survey of Manufacturing," *Quarterly Journal of Economics* 109 (1994): 367-97.

Björnerstedt, J. and J.W. Weibull, "Nash Equilibrium and Evolution by Imitation," In *The Rational Foundations of Economic Behavior*; Arrow, K.J., Colombatto, E., Perlman, M., Schmidt, C., Eds. (St. Martin's Press: New York, 1996); pp. 155--181.

Blackmore, S. *The Meme Machine*, Oxford; Oxford University Press, 1999.

Brock, W. A., and Malliaris, A. G. (1989), *Differential Equations, Stability, and Chaos in Dynamical Economics*, North Holland, Amsterdam, Netherlands.

Border, Kim. *Fixed point theorems with applications to economics and game theory*. Cambridge University Press, 1985. Reprinted version 1999.

Bowles, Samuel. "Institutional Poverty Traps", in *Poverty Traps*, Samuel Bowles, Steven N. Durlauf and Karla Hoff eds., Princeton, Princeton University Press, 2006.

Cimoli, M., Ferraz J. C. and A. Primi, "Science,Technology and Innovation Policies in Global Open Economies: Reflections from Latin America and the Caribbean," *Journal Globalization, Competitiveness & Governability* 3 (2009).

Cooper, R., and A. John, "Coordinating coordination failures in keynesian models," *Quarterly Journal of Economics* 103 (1998): 441-63.

Durlauf, S., "A Theory of Persistent Income Inequality," *Journal of Economic Growth* 1 (1996): 75-93.

—. "The Memberships Theory of Inequality: Ideas and Implications," in *Elites, Minorities, and Economic Growth*, E. Brezis and P. Temin, eds., Amsterdam: North Holland, 1999.

—. "The Memberships Theory of Poverty: The Role of Group Affiliations in Determining Socioeconomic Outcomes," in *Understanding Poverty in America*, S. Danziger and R. Haveman eds., Cambridge: Cambridge: Harvard University Press, 2001.

—. "Neighborhood Effects," Madison, University of Wisconsin, Department of Economics, SSRI working paper 2003-17 (prepared for J. Vernon Henderson and Jacques-François Thisse eds., *Handbook of Regional and Urban Economics*, vol. 4, 2003).

Eldredge, N. and Stephen J. Gould., "Punctuated Equilibria: An Alternative to Phyletic Gradualism," In Schopf, Thomas J.M. (ed.), *Models in Paleobiology*, pp. 82-115. Freeman, Cooper and Co., San Francisco, 1972.

Fudenberg D, and D. Levine, "Self-Confirming Equilibrium and the Lucas Critique," the *Journal of Economic Theory,* 2007:

Fudenberg D, and J. Tirole, *Game Theory*, The MIT Press, 1991.

Funk, P. and Vogel, T., "Endogenous Skill Bias," *Journal of Economic Dynamics and Control* 28 (2004): 2155-93.

Gaunersdorfer, A. J. Hofbauer and K. Sigmund, "On the Dynamics of Assymetric Games," *Theoretical Population Biology* 39 (1991): 345-357.

Gintis, H. *Game Theory Evolving*, Second Edition, Princeton University Press, 2009.

Greif, A. "Cultural Beliefs and the Organization of the Society: A Historical and Theoretical Reflection on Collectivist and Individualist Societies," *Journal of Political Economy* 102 (1994): 912-950.

Haskel, J.E. and Heden, Y., "Computers and the Demand for Skilled Labour: Industry and Establishment-level Panel Evidence for the UK," *Economic Journal* 109 (1999): C68-C79.

Hendricks, L. "Equipment investment and growth in developing countries," *Journal of Development Economics* 61 (2000): 335-364.

Hofbauer, J. and K. Sigmund, *Evolutionary Games and Population Dynamics*, Cambridge University Press, 2002.

Hofbauer, J. Schuster, P. and Sigmund, K. "A note on evolutionary stable strategies and game dynamics," *Journal of Theoretical Biology* 81 (1979): 609-612.

Hoff, K., "Beyond Rosenstein-Rodan: The Modern Theory of Coordination Problems in Development," *Annual World Bank Conference on Development*. The World Bank, 2001: 145-176.

Hornstein, A., P. Krusell and G.L. Violante, "The Effects of technical Change on Labor Market Inequalities," in Aghion, P. and Durlauf, S. (eds.) *Handbook of Economic Growth*, Elsevier, 2005.

Kiley M.T., "The Supply of Skilled Labour and Skill-biased Technological Progress," *Economic Journal* 109 (1999): 708-24.

Kopinak, K. "Gender As a Vehicle for the Subordination of Women Maquiladora Workers in Mexico," in *Latin American Perspectives* 22 (1995): 30-48.

Krugman, P. *Development, Geography and Economic Theory*. MIT Press, 1995.

Lavezzi, A. "On High-Skill and Low-Skill Equilibria: a Markov Chain Approach," *Metroeconomica* 57 (2006): 121-157.

Lucas, R. "On the Mechanics of Economic Development," *Journal of Monetary Economics* 22 (1988): 3-42.

Machin, S. and Van Reenen, J. "Technology and Changes in the Skill Structure: Evidence from Seven OECD Countries," *Quarterly Journal of Economics* 113 (1998): 1215-44.

Maloney, F. W. and G. Perry, "Towards an efficient innovation policy in Latin America," *CEPAL Review* (2005).

Mankiw, N.; Romer, D.; and Weil, D. "A contribution of the empirics economic growth," *The Quarterly Journal of Economics* 107 (1992): 407-37.

Maynard Smith, J., *On Evolution*. Edinburgh University Press, 1972.

Maynard Smith, J. and Price, G.R. "The Logic of Animal Conflict," *Nature* 246 (1973): 15-18.

Maynard Smith, J. "The theory of games and the evolution of animal conflict," *Journal of Theoretical Biology* 47 (1974): 209-22.

—. *Evolution and the Theory of Games*, Cambridge University Press, 1982.

Nachbar, J. H. "Evolutionary selection in dynamic games," *International Journal of Game Theory* 19 (1990): 59-90.

Nelson, R.; Phelps, E. "Investment in Humans, Technological Diffusion, and Economic Growth," *American Economic Review* 61 (1966): 69-75.

Polterovich, V. "Institutional Trap," *The New Palgrave Dictionary of Economics*, Eds. Steven N. Durlauf and Lawrence E. Blume, Palgrave Macmillan, 2008.

Poulsen, Anders and Svendsen, G., "Social capital and endogenous preferences," *Public Choice* 123 (2005): 171-196.

Redding, S. "The Low-Skill, Low-Quality Trap: Strategic Complementarities between Human Capital and R&D," *Economic Journal* 106 (1996): 458-70.

Romer, P. "Increasing Returns and Long-Run Economic Growth" *Journal of Political Economy* 94 (1986): 1002-1037.

Ros, J. *Development Theory and Economics of Growths*, The University of Michigan Press, 2000.

Salamon, L. *The Tools of governement: Aguide to the new governance.* Oxford University Press, 2002.

Sanchez Carrera, E. "Imitation and evolutionary stability of poverty Traps", *Journal of Bioeconomics* 14 (2012): 1-20.

Santiago-Rodriguez, F. and L. Alcorta, "Complementary human resource management and development practices and innovation: assessing existing methodologies from a Mexican perspective," Paper presented at the DRUID-DIME Academy Winter 2006. PhD Conference: The Evolution of Capabilities and Industrial Dynamics Hotel Comwell Rebild Bakker; Skørping, Denmark; January 26-28, 2006.

Sandler, T. and Tschirhart, J. "Club theory: Thirty years later" *Public Choice* 93 (1997): 335-355.

Sanditov, B. "Essays on Social Learning and Imitation," Ph.D. thesis, Maastricht University, 2006.

Schlag, K. H. "Why Imitate, and if so, How? A Boundedly Rational Approach to Multi-Armed Bandits," *Journal of Economic Theory* 78 (1998): 130-156.

—. "Which One Should I Imitate," *Journal of Mathematical Economics* 31 (1999): 493-522.

Schultz, T.W. "The value of the ability to deal with disequilibria," *Journal of Economic Literature* 13 (1975): 827-846.

Selten, R. "Reexamination of the Perfectness Concept for Equilibrium Points in Extensive Games," *International Journal of Game Theory* 4 (1975): 25-55.

Selten, R. "A note on evolutionarily stable strategies in asymmetrical animal conflicts," *Journal of Theoretical Biology* 84 (1980): 93-101.

Shone, R. *Economic Dynamics*. China Renmin University Press, 2003.

Stiglitz, J. "Towrad a New Paradigm for Development: Strategies, Policies, and Processes" in *UNCTAD, Prebisch Lecture*, 1998.

Stiglitz, J. and Hoff, K. "Modern Economic Theory Development," in *Frontiers of Development Economics*. Oxford University Press, 2001.

Stockey N. "Human Capital, Product Quality and Growth," *The Quarterly Journal of Economics* 106 (1991): 587-616.

Taylor, P.D. and L.B. Jonker, "Evolutionary Stable Strategies and Game Dynamics", *Math. Biosci.*, 40 (1978): 145-156.

Taylor, P. "Evolutionarily Stable Strategies with Two Types of Player," *Journal of Applied Probability* 16 (1979): 76-83.

Vonortas, N. "Building competitive firms: technology policy initiatives in Latin America," *Technology in Society* 24 (2002): 433-59.

Van Damme, E. *Stability and Perfection of Nash Equilibria*, Springer-Verlag, 1991.

Vega-Redondo, F. *Evolution, Games, and Economic Behavior*, Oxford University Press, 1996.

—. "The evolution of Walrasian behavior," *Econometrica* 65 (1997): 375--384.

Weibull, W. J. *Evolutionary Game Theory*, The MIT Press, 1995.

Zeeman, A. C. "Population Dynamics from Game Theory," in *Global Theory of Dynamical Systems.* Z. Nitecki and C. Robinson, eds., pp. 471-497. Springer-Verlag. Lecture Notes in Mathematics 819, 1992.